Firestone Books
Success Begins Here

A Christmas Carol Revision Guide for GCSE

This guide is also dyslexia-friendly!

Emma Larard

Series Editor: Nicola Walsh

Firestone Books' no-nonsense guides have all you need
to do brilliantly at your English Literature GCSE

firestonebooks.com

A Christmas Carol: Revision Guide for GCSE
Dyslexia-Friendly Edition
Emma Larard

This dyslexia-friendly edition has a large easy-to-read font, minimal italics and capital letters, large line spacing, and is printed on cream paper – all combining to ensure an easier reading experience.

Series Editor: Nicola Walsh

2021 Edition

ISBN-13: 9781909608429

Published by Firestone Books

firestonebooks.com

You can stay up to date by following Firestone Books on Facebook and Twitter, or subscribing to our fabulous newsletter.

~ Contents ~

Background information

The novella – summary and analysis

Form, structure and language

Key quotations and glossary

Revision and exam help

Our fabulous new revision guides are out now!

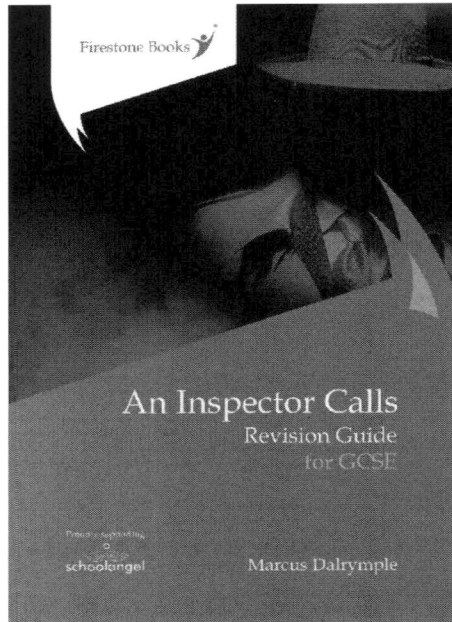

Revision Guides for GCSE

- Dr Jekyll and Mr Hyde
- An Inspector Calls
- Macbeth
- English Language

25 Key Quotations for GCSE

- Romeo and Juliet
- A Christmas Carol
- Macbeth
- Dr Jekyll and Mr Hyde
- An Inspector Calls

But that's not all! We've also got a host of annotation-friendly editions, containing oodles of space for you to fill with those all-important notes:

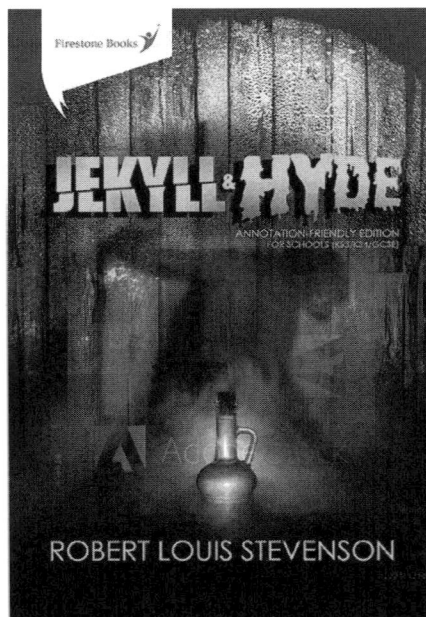

Annotation-Friendly Editions

- Dr Jekyll and Mr Hyde
- A Christmas Carol
- Romeo and Juliet
- Macbeth
  … and lots more!

And we've got **all** these books available in super-helpful **dyslexia-friendly** and **large print** editions too!

Available through Amazon, Waterstones, and all good bookshops!

Quick tip: when you see an asterisk after a word, it means you can find the word or phrase in the glossary on page 95 of this book.

~ Background information ~

Charles Dickens

Dickens seriously believed in social responsibility* – he thought the rich should help support the poor and that education was the key to raising the living standards of those in poverty. Charity was important to Dickens, not only at Christmas but all year round. In Stave Five Scrooge says he will "'honour Christmas in my heart, and try to keep it all the year'". It comes as no surprise then that Dickens himself experienced poverty when he worked in a factory when he was just twelve years old.

If all this focus on social improvement wasn't enough to give us a high opinion of the author, Dickens is also credited with making our Christmas celebrations what they are today. Family dinners, fun games and supporting those who are less fortunate are all traditions that Dickens values in A Christmas Carol.

The novel is a timeless classic which sold more than 5,000 copies by Christmas Eve when it was first published on the 17th of December in 1843. At the time this was a huge number of books, showing that it was instantly a popular story.

Biography

- Dickens was born in 1812 in Portsmouth, England where he spent a happy childhood.

- However, the family moved to London where his father was transferred for work when Dickens was nine years old.

- In 1824, his father was sent to prison for debt, so the young Dickens worked in a boot polish factory for two years to support his family. This is where Dickens' empathy* with the poor began as he knew what it was like to work as a child in horrific conditions in a factory.

- Despite having little formal education, in 1827 Dickens began work in an office for a solicitor before becoming a court reporter and then a writer.

- In 1836, he married Catherine Hogarth and they had ten children.

- In the same year, his first novel was published and he became a popular, successful writer.

- In 1843, A Christmas Carol, which was written in response to a government report on child labour, was published. Dickens felt upset about the terrible effects that working in a factory had on children so he wanted to raise awareness of their suffering by writing a story about them.

- He decided to write a ghost story, which was a popular genre at the time, with a strong moral but a happy ending.

- During his life, Dickens wrote over 20 novels including Oliver Twist and Great Expectations.

- He died in 1870, aged 58, and is buried in Westminster Abbey.

The Industrial revolution* and poverty

Until the 1760s, Britain's economy was based on agriculture and farming, and most employment was in farming jobs in the countryside. Many people owned small farms and lived off their own land, growing crops and vegetables, and rearing animals for meat, eggs and dairy produce. Others worked for the local landowners as farm labourers. However, that all changed when a large number of factories, mainly producing cloth, sprung up in cities, mostly in London. With a population growth from around one million to six million people between 1800 and 1900, London became the heart of the country's economy. In 1841 it was the biggest city in the world and was the place to be for business, government and finance. This time period became known as The Industrial Revolution*.

This sudden growth had significant consequences though. On the plus side, factory owners made a lot of money; however, many factory workers experienced extreme poverty. Many of the wealthy factory owners exploited their workers by forcing them to work long hours but paid them very little money. As the rich got richer, the poor got poorer. One ghost in the novella 'cried piteously at being unable to assist a wretched woman with an infant, whom it saw below, upon a door-step'. The poor woman and her child portray the effects of poverty that people experienced as a consequence of working in terrible conditions in a factory. The ghost feels guilty for not helping people like them when it was alive, showing how pitiful and unhappy the mother and child must look to move him to feel so terrible about his actions.

With such a huge population increase people were forced to live in overcrowded, cramped conditions where lots of them suffered from diseases such as cholera*. Dickens demonstrates these conditions in the novella when he describes a poverty-stricken area of London: 'The ways were foul and narrow; the shops and houses wretched; the people half-naked, drunken, slipshod, ugly. Alleys and archways, like so many cesspools, disgorged their offences of smell, and dirt, and life, upon the straggling streets; and the whole quarter reeked with crime, with filth, and misery.' For the poor, London was a filthy and smelly city, where people were forced to steal and beg in order to stay alive.

In the 1800s, children were not treated the way they are today. Some were forced to work for more than twelve hour days, six days a week, in a dangerous, noisy factory. Dickens personifies the effect of the poor treatment of child factory workers through the two children, Ignorance* and Want*, whom the Ghost of Christmas Present hides in his robes. Dickens makes his description of their appearance so shocking in order to show what a lack of education and support from the richer people in society can do: 'It brought two children; wretched, abject, frightful, hideous, miserable.' The horrible living and working conditions did not just affect the adults, it also affected the children too.

Something needed to be done but everyone seemed to have a different opinion on the best way to prevent poverty. Dickens believed that rich people with a high status in society should help by donating money so that those living in poverty could have access to food, clothing and shelter. He also believed that the government should do more to ensure poor children gained a better education. Dickens felt the factory owners should not exploit their workers and should pay them a fair wage so they could afford to live in better conditions. The reader sees all of Dickens' beliefs clearly in the novella.

The 1834 New Poor Law

However, the economist Thomas Robert Malthus' ideas on poverty were pretty barbaric compared to what Dickens believed. Malthus thought that overpopulation should be reduced through famine and disease, which would leave enough food and resources for the rest of the population. In other words, poor people should be left to die. Malthus believed the poor were given too much financial assistance from the government, which came from taxes that were paid by people in the higher classes. He believed that able-bodied people should work for their money and not be able to claim any support.

Dickens demonstrates this view through Scrooge who has the same attitude when the charity collectors ask him to donate money to the poor: 'If they would rather die…they had better do it, and decrease the surplus population.' Scrooge believes it would be better for poor people to die because if the population increases then there won't be enough food for everyone. He thinks that poor people don't deserve to be given support by the government and the higher classes because they are not contributing anything to help the country make money. Through Scrooge, Dickens suggests that there are people in society who do not understand what it is like to live in poverty and that they need to change their attitude and have more sympathy.

In 1834, the government passed the New Poor Law* which meant unemployed people had to enter a workhouse* if they wanted food and shelter. Although this sounds like a reasonable deal, in reality conditions in the workhouses were horrific and brutal in order to stop people from relying on the government for support.

But many wealthy people, like Scrooge, believed this was the right place for poor people, who they felt were lazy. Scrooge refuses to financially support those in poverty as he believes the government is already doing that: "'Are there no prisons?... And the Union workhouses? Are they still in operation?...The Treadmill* and the Poor Law are in full vigour, then?'". Here, Dickens lists all the types of support that the government is giving to the poor, but these did not help to get people out of poverty.

But not everyone agreed with the Poor Law. Dickens felt that education was the key to helping people out of poverty. He supported the Ragged Schools, which were founded in 1844 with the aim of providing a free education for destitute* children living in London. Not only did they provide an education, but also food and clothing for families who could not afford it. Dickens believed that these schools meant children would gain skills and knowledge and as a consequence they would be more likely to get better jobs and therefore earn more money to support themselves.

Dickens directly criticises the 1834 New Poor Law and the government when he describes the phantoms* that fill the air, regretting their failure to support the poor when they were alive: 'some few (they might be guilty governments) were linked together; none were free.' Dickens believed the government should do more to give financial assistance to those living in poverty because it wasn't their fault that they were born into hardship with little opportunity to improve their chances in life.

Religion in the Victorian era

In the 19th century, most people were very religious, especially those in the middle and upper classes. The majority of people at the time were Christian and about half of the population attended church on a Sunday.

However, their interpretations of Christianity differed. Some people were very strict about always doing what they thought was right and behaving correctly. They didn't drink alcohol or have sex, and attended church every week. Other people focused more on the Christian concepts of giving, charity and supporting those who are less fortunate. Dickens believed that it wasn't necessary to behave correctly all the time but that it was important to help those living in poverty.

Sabbatarianism* is the belief that Sunday is a holy day when no one should work. In the Victorian times, this had a significant impact on those who were poor because on the one day they were not working in the factories, there were no shops open for them. This included the bakeries where their food was cooked because they did not have ovens at home, so they were denied a proper meal on their one day of rest. Dickens was opposed to this strict law. In the novella, Scrooge says that the law prevents poor people from experiencing '"innocent enjoyment"' and that they are deprived of '"their means of dining every seventh day, often the only day on which they can be said to dine at all"'. Because the poor can't go to the bakers on a Sunday, Scrooge says it is unfair that they are unable to enjoy a hot dinner on their one day off work, which is exactly how Dickens felt.

Victorian readers would have recognised Tiny Tim as the heroic and patient physically disabled child who was used in literature to provoke sympathy in readers. He not only gracefully accepts his situation but believes that his disability can help others keep their faith. He makes his father proud when he says he 'hoped the people saw him in church, because he was a cripple, and it might be pleasant to them to remember upon Christmas Day, who made lame* beggars walk and blind men see'. Dickens makes the reader feel sympathy for Tiny Tim so that they want to follow and act on the Christian belief that people should be charitable towards the poor.

The supernatural*

However, some people were becoming less religious in the 19th century due to advances in science and technology, which meant that religious ideas were proven to be incorrect. In addition, people's beliefs in ghosts and spiritualism* were increasing. Although it is said that Dickens didn't believe in ghosts himself, he was fascinated with other people's thoughts about the supernatural.

Ghosts appeared in books before the Victorian times, but the ghost story genre was invented by the Victorians. They enjoyed reading stories about the supernatural, and with several ghosts and a non-chronological* timescale, A Christmas Carol definitely ticks this box. Dickens' message, that wealthy people should take more responsibility for helping the poor people in society, is conveyed through these ghosts. Like Marley, they are all destined to roam the earth regretting their actions of not supporting the poor when they were alive: 'The air was filled with phantoms, wandering hither and thither in restless haste, and moaning as they went.' Dickens uses the supernatural as a warning to the middle and upper class members of society to act more morally towards the poor to avoid being punished in the afterlife.

Dickens' Christmas

One of the novella's key messages, that the festive season should be a time of goodwill, generosity and family, has had a significant impact on our Christmas today. In the early Victorian times, Christmas was barely celebrated, however by the end of the 19th century it had become a very important occasion. This was also a time when Christmas cards, crackers, carols and Christmas dinner were growing in popularity.

Dickens' novella inspired the way we see Christmas today:

- The Ghost of Christmas Present is similar to our Father Christmas: 'there sat a jolly Giant… It was clothed in one simple green robe, or mantle, bordered with white fur.'

- The feast the ghost sits among is similar to the Christmas dinners we serve today: 'turkeys, geese, game, poultry, brawn, great joints of meat, sucking-pigs, long wreaths if sausages, mince-pies, plum-puddings, barrels of oysters, red-hot chestnuts, cherry-cheeked apples, juicy oranges, luscious pears, immense twelfth cakes.'

In Victorian times, beef or goose were usually eaten at Christmas. These meats were cheaper than turkey, which was seen as a luxury that only the more affluent* people in society could afford. When Scrooge decides to buy the 'prize turkey' from the poulterer's to send to Bob Cratchit, he is being incredibly generous.

Dickens himself enjoyed parties, feasts and games at Christmas and this is reflected in the celebrations held by Fred and Mr Fezziwig:

- At Scrooge's nephew Fred's house, Christmas is a time of great excitement: 'After a while they played at forfeits; for it is good to be children sometimes, and never better than at Christmas.'

- At Mr Fezziwig's, Christmas is also a time of generosity and celebration: 'There were more dances, and there were forfeits, and more dances and there was cake…and plenty of beer.'

Christmas was becoming more secular*, which means not connected with religion. Dickens believed this was good for society as Christmas was becoming a time for family, happiness and celebrations rather than strict rules such as attending church on Christmas Day and not drinking alcohol. However, he still wanted people to follow the Christian belief that they should show generosity and goodwill towards the poor at this time of year.

When he wrote A Christmas Carol, Dickens' overall purpose was to highlight the consequences of poverty in Victorian England and to encourage his readers to be more generous and charitable, not only at Christmas but all year round.

Progress and revision check

1. What time of year did Dickens believe charity was important?
2. Where did Dickens work when he was just twelve years old?
3. What inspired Dickens to write A Christmas Carol?
4. What was the time period called when Britain's economy changed from agriculture and farming to factory work?
5. What were the consequences of rapid population growth in London?
6. Who was the economist who believed starvation would solve poverty?
7. Which law did the government pass to attempt to control poverty?
8. What is Sabbatarianism?
9. What type of stories did the Victorians enjoy reading?
10. Which Christmas traditions grew in popularity at the end of the 19th century?

~ The novella – summary and analysis ~

Who's who

Main characters

Ebenezer Scrooge is the protagonist* of the novella. He is a creditor (someone who lends money) and owns a counting house. The story is about how he changes from being a miserly*, avaricious* old man who likes being alone, to a caring, generous person who wants to support people who are less fortunate in society.

Jacob Marley was Scrooge's business partner who died seven years before the story begins. When he was alive, he also thought wealth and profit were important. Marley's ghost visits Scrooge to warn him that if he does not change his ways he will suffer the same fate as Marley, to roam the earth forever as a remorseful spirit.

Fred is Scrooge's nephew and his sister Fan's son. He is a jolly, positive character who is friendly to everyone and he wants Scrooge to be part of his family. Fred represents people in society who are kind and generous and this contrasts with Scrooge.

The Cratchits are a lower class Victorian family who have very little money but are happy. The father, Bob, is Scrooge's clerk, and is paid poorly. Bob is a caring family man who has a close relationship with his son Tiny Tim.

Tiny Tim, Bob Cratchit's son, is a disabled young boy who is positive about his condition and very religious. His character represents the poor people who suffered from poverty in Victorian England and how they are real people with real feelings.

The Ghost of Christmas Past has the appearance of a child and an old man at the same time. The ghost shows Scrooge his past and how he once was a happy person who formed loving relationships and how his focus on money caused him to change.

The Ghost of Christmas Present has the appearance of a jolly giant wearing festive clothes and is surrounded by traditional Christmas food and decorations. He shows Scrooge how other people, both rich and poor, celebrate Christmas.

The Ghost of Christmas Yet To Come is silent and wears a black hood covering its face. The ghost shows Scrooge the depressing future, which will happen if he does not change his ways and become more charitable and thoughtful.

Minor characters

Fan is Scrooge's sister and Fred's mother, who died when she was a young woman. Fan was cheerful and loving, and she and Scrooge had a close relationship.

Mr Fezziwig was Scrooge's boss when he was a young apprentice. He is a kind and generous man who cares about all of his employees.

Ignorance* and Want* are two children, a boy and a girl, who represent poverty in Victorian England. They are not real characters but they symbolise* the problems that cause poverty, which are lack of education, food, clothing and a warm place to live.

Belle was Scrooge's fiancée. She ended their engagement because she felt Scrooge had changed and had become obsessed with profit and wealth.

The Novella

Preface – Dickens' message for the reader

Dickens directly addresses the reader and tells them that he has written this story to convey a message which he hopes will not make them upset at Christmas time.

Analysis

Dickens uses the first person and speaks as himself to introduce his story. He says it is a 'Ghostly little book' and he hopes it may 'haunt [the reader's] house pleasantly'. He also says it will include a 'Ghost of an Idea' which tells the reader the novella is an allegory* so that they know it will include characters and events which are symbols* used to convey his important message. However, Dickens is eager to point out that he wants his story to entertain people rather than preach to them.

Stave One – Marley's Ghost visits Scrooge

On Christmas Eve, Ebenezer Scrooge and his clerk Bob Cratchit are working in a freezing cold office which Scrooge refuses to heat because he is so miserly*. Fred, his nephew, visits the office to ask Scrooge to join his family for Christmas. Scrooge refuses his invitation, saying that he hates everything about Christmas. He also rejects the requests of the 'two portly* gentlemen' to give money to charity and sends away a young boy who attempts to sing a Christmas carol.

Later that night, when Scrooge is in his dark and dingy home, he is visited by Marley's ghost who is chained by padlocks and money-boxes. Marley's ghost warns Scrooge that if he continues to be so tight with his money he will suffer the same fate as him, which is to not have any rest in the afterlife because he was so obsessed with money. He tells Scrooge that three spirits will visit him to help him change.

Analysis

Scrooge is introduced

The narrator introduces Scrooge, the protagonist* of the novella, as a 'squeezing, wrenching, grasping, scraping, clutching, covetous old sinner*', so that from the beginning the reader dislikes Scrooge and understands that he is not generous with his money. This is also emphasised when we learn that Scrooge doesn't like Christmas and believes people have no reason to celebrate as it costs too much money.

Scrooge's home life is miserable: he eats a 'melancholy dinner in his usual melancholy tavern' and lives in 'a gloomy suite of rooms'. He is also miserly at home, as the 'very low fire' shows how he doesn't want to spend money on heating. Dickens shows that Scrooge isn't just a tight businessman focused on profit but that his whole life revolves around being selfish and greedy, which makes the reader question whether he really is capable of such a dramatic change.

The weather sets the mood

Dickens uses pathetic fallacy* when he describes the fog to create a sense of gloom and mystery: 'the fog came pouring in at every chink and keyhole.' This represents how people who share Scrooge's negative, miserly attitude are everywhere and need to change. As the charity collectors leave Scrooge's office, the 'fog and darkness thickened' suggesting that Scrooge's life has become darker and he is even blinder to the poor because he has rejected any attempts to help them.

Scrooge's interactions with others

When Fred enters the office with a warm, friendly attitude and 'cheerful voice', we see that he is a direct contrast to his uncle Scrooge, to show

how some people are full of the Christmas spirit, want to be charitable in the festive season and want to spend time with family. Similarly, we see how rude and unfriendly Scrooge is when he rejects the charity collectors' requests for a donation. Scrooge has strong opinions about how the poor are 'idle' and that the government already makes provisions for them in the workhouses*, reinforcing his selfish nature and how he believes he is right.

Scrooge treats his clerk poorly

Dickens invites us into Scrooge's workplace where we see how badly he treats his clerk, Bob, in his 'dismal little cell', with 'one coal', which shows how stingy Scrooge is with the heating. When the first conversation takes place between Scrooge and his 'clerk', he is nameless, in order to give a sense that he is Scrooge's employee whom Scrooge controls. By giving him a name later in the novella, Dickens increases our sympathy for him because he seems more like a real person with real feelings.

Similarly, in their conversation about the 'clerk' having Christmas Day off work, Dickens uses direct speech for Scrooge, such as "'it's not convenient'", whereas he uses reported speech for the clerk: 'the clerk observed that it was only once a year.' This creates a sense of the clerk's inferiority*; that he is less important than Scrooge and does not have a voice, and that Scrooge has authority over him as he is his employer who is in charge. This reflects how Dickens believed that the poor were also voiceless in society and it was the upper and middle classes that had control.

Marley's ghost arrives

The first supernatural element of the story is introduced when Scrooge sees 'not a knocker, but Marley's face' on his door, foreshadowing* more mysterious events. The reader is now on edge, so Dickens increases the dramatic tension by using the sense of sound. When Scrooge closes the door the 'sound resounded through the house like thunder' and he hears a 'clanking noise, deep down below'. This makes the reader feel even more tense and aware that there are negative events to follow.

Marley's ghost dramatically enters and drags with him a long chain of 'cash-boxes, keys, padlocks, ledgers, deeds and heavy purses'. These objects, which are linked to money, symbolise how focused Marley was on wealth and profit when he was alive and how he is now being weighed down by the guilt of his selfishness. Marley is full of remorse for not taking responsibility for helping those in poverty and is now suffering the consequences: "'I cannot rest, I cannot stay, I cannot linger anywhere.'"

Stave Two – The First Spirit shows Scrooge his past

The Ghost of Christmas Past shows Scrooge how lonely he was when he was a young boy as he was the only child left at school at Christmas time. However, we also see happy memories such as his close relationship with his sister Fan who was very excited to see him when she came to collect him from school. The spirit then shows Scrooge the keen, enthusiastic young man he once was when he was an apprentice at his kind employer Mr Fezziwig's Christmas party.

Next, Scrooge witnesses the conversation between him and Belle when she ended their engagement because money was more important to him than their relationship. Scrooge also sees Belle as a grown woman with her family and realises his attitude towards money and towards others in society means he has missed the chance to have a family of his own.

~ The novella – summary and analysis ~

Analysis

The Ghost of Christmas Past arrives

Dickens emphasises the supernatural element of the story when Scrooge hears the church bell strike twelve even though it was 'past two when he went to bed'. This gives a sense of mystery and indicates that everything is not as it seems. Tension is built before the first ghost's arrival through the detailed description of Scrooge's confusion about the time, and the countdown to the bell chiming one o'clock: 'Ding dong! "A quarter past," said Scrooge, counting.' Dickens also makes the reader wait to see what will appear which creates suspense and makes them nervously anticipate the ghost's arrival.

When the Ghost of Christmas Past appears next to Scrooge's bed, it emits* a 'bright clear jet of light' which Scrooge wants it to cover. This represents his reluctance to face up to the reality of his actions in the past, which the ghost is about to show him. Similarly, the stave ends with Scrooge battling with the ghost to cover the 'high and bright' light it emits, which represents the way the ghost has exposed his past and made him feel emotional and traumatised by the reality of the truth; Scrooge has realised how happy he used to be and how his life has revolved around money which means he has sacrificed relationships with family and friends.

Scrooge feels emotional about his childhood

When the ghost takes Scrooge back to his childhood the setting immediately contrasts to London: 'a little market town appeared…with its bridge, its church and winding river.' The gentle, happy atmosphere shows Scrooge once had a very different life where he was content. We see a hint of Scrooge beginning to change as he is 'filled with gladness' when he sees his young friends wishing each other a Merry Christmas. Similarly, when the ghost shows Scrooge himself as a 'solitary* child, neglected by his friends', we see Scrooge becoming very sad, an emotion that he hasn't shown in adulthood because he didn't want to remember how he was isolated by his friends and was rejected by his father as a child.

Scrooge's sees his past relationships

Scrooge once had a close, loving relationship with his sister Fan, who persuaded their father to collect Scrooge from school so that they could spend Christmas together as a family. This foreshadows* Scrooge's change as Fan says their father is '"much kinder"' which implies Scrooge has the potential to be kind too. The siblings' closeness is emphasised through Fan's excitement that they will be spending Christmas together, showing how Scrooge was once close to someone in his family.

Mr Fezziwig's Christmas party shows Scrooge how his former employer created happiness by being kind and generous towards his employees and not through spending lots of money: '"the happiness he gives is quite great, as if it cost a fortune."' The ghost shows this scene to Scrooge to make him realise how badly he treats his employee Bob Cratchit and how he could be more generous and kind, like his old boss Mr Fezziwig was to him when he worked for him as a young apprentice.

Belle shows Scrooge what he has lost

When Belle says that she is ending their engagement because money has become Scrooge's 'idol*', we see how Scrooge appeared to value money more than family which has left him without children of his own. Dickens emphasises the family life that Scrooge has missed out on by describing the children who surround Belle as a 'flushed and boisterous group' and who bring happiness to the older Belle. This contrasts to Belle's husband's description of Scrooge when he sees him in his office, as "'quite alone in the world'". Dickens juxtaposes* the two scenes to emphasise Scrooge's isolation and loneliness because he rejected people for money.

Stave Three –
The Second Spirit shows families celebrating Christmas

The Ghost of Christmas Present arrives and shows Scrooge all the extravagant, rich food and décor that people enjoy at Christmas time. He then shows Scrooge the Cratchit family celebrating Christmas happily together, even though they have very little money. Here, Scrooge discovers that the disabled Tiny Tim will die if the future does not change and he is very upset by this news.

At Fred's house, his family are enjoying games and festivities. They mock Scrooge for hating Christmas but Fred says he feels sorry for his uncle. Finally, the spirit shows Scrooge two poor children, Ignorance and Want, who are hidden in the ghost's clothes. He warns Scrooge that it is society's responsibility to help people who are less fortunate than themselves so that poverty does not become an even bigger problem.

Analysis

The Ghost of Christmas Present arrives

When Scrooge first sees the ghost it is sitting in a room with plenty of festive food and traditional Christmas decorations. Similarly, Dickens describes in detail the amount of food that is available in the shops at Christmas time and uses a simile* to emphasise the cheerful atmosphere, describing chestnuts that were 'like the waistcoats of jolly old gentlemen'. Dickens wants to convey how, at Christmas time, having an abundance* of food and decorations should not just be for the rich in society and that it should be shared with those who are not able to afford such luxuries.

The ghost shows Scrooge that Christmas is worth celebrating because it makes people happy, despite the freezing cold conditions, as there is 'an air of cheerfulness' in the streets. The ghost has the ability to stop people arguing, as when it sees them speaking angrily to each other it sprinkles them with water from its torch and 'good humour was restored'. The ghost is showing Scrooge the benefits of being full of the Christmas spirit and how it leads to generosity and kindness.

Scrooge blames the ghost for those in poverty not being able to have a cooked meal on a Sunday, as the bakeries are shut due to the Christian belief that Sunday is a day of rest. He says the ghost does not allow them an '"opportunity of innocent enjoyment"'. However, the ghost responds that some people behave selfishly and say they are a Christian but actually it does not believe they are acting correctly. Dickens wants to show how people who are strictly Christian are not thinking about what is best for everyone in society by following strict rules such as Sabbatarianism*.

The Cratchits' Christmas

When the ghost takes Scrooge to the Cratchits' 'four-roomed house', it wants to show him the reality of living in poverty, but also how happy the family are despite their lack of money. The atmosphere in the Cratchits' home is in direct contrast to Scrooge's lonely, quiet house. On Christmas Day, everyone in the Cratchit family takes a role: 'Mrs Cratchit made the gravy…; Master Peter mashed the potatoes…; Miss Belinda sweetened the apple sauce; Martha dusted the hot plates…; the two young Cratchits set chairs for everybody.' Dickens uses a long sentence to create a pacey rhythm to demonstrate how lively and busy the house is and to show how much everyone eagerly gets involved in the preparations.

Dickens also uses foreshadowing* when he says Bob held Tiny Tim's hand as if he 'dreaded that he might be taken from him', which hints to the reader that Tiny Tim will die. Dickens does this to make the reader consider the consequences of not helping poor people like the Cratchits. Watching the family celebrate Christmas, Scrooge realises that poverty is not just an inconvenient issue but something that affects real people. The reader can see that he is well on the path to redemption* because he cares intensely about what will happen to Tiny Tim in the future.

Fred's party shows how family is important

When the ghost and Scrooge visit Fred's Christmas party we see another family who are enjoying the celebrations. However, here we see a family who have money to spend at Christmas time, highlighting the difference between the wealthy and the poor. Dickens uses repetition to refer to Fred as 'Scrooge's nephew' and his wife as 'Scrooge's niece', to emphasise how Scrooge has a family but he is missing out on being part of it because he has rejected them. Fred's family mock Scrooge for his negative attitude towards Christmas; however, Fred defends him and says that he is '"a comical fellow"' but only hurts himself by being miserly, and concludes that he pities him. Dickens does this to show the reader that Fred is a forgiving and loving character. He is everything that Scrooge could be if he chose to change.

Both families raise a toast to Scrooge's health, showing their goodwill towards him, despite his behaviour towards them. This thoughtfulness by both families contrasts significantly with his selfishness. Dickens intentionally juxtaposes the celebratory Christmas scenes with the sudden appearance of the poverty-stricken children Ignorance and Want from the ghost's robes. He aims to shock the reader so that they realise that although Christmas is a happy time for many, the reality is that some people are living on the brink of death.

Stave Four –
The Third Spirit shows Scrooge what could happen in the future

The Ghost of Christmas Yet To Come shows Scrooge how several people, including some rich businessmen, do not care about an unknown man who has died. The spirit shows an undertaker's man*, a charwoman* and a laundress* selling the dead man's possessions in a poor part of town to a man who trades stolen goods. They have been able to steal from him because the charwoman was his cleaner, the laundress washed his clothes and the man was the assistant to the person arranging the funeral. Scrooge then sees a young couple, who owe the dead man money, who are relieved he has died because he was putting them under a lot of pressure to pay back money they didn't have.

However, Scrooge then observes the Cratchit family's devastation after the death of Tiny Tim. Bob is especially affected by the loss of his son. Next, the spirit shows Scrooge a gravestone with his name on it, revealing that the dead man is Scrooge and this is what will happen if he does not change his ways. Scrooge promises to learn from the lessons of the three spirits and become a generous, kind and charitable person.

Analysis

The Ghost of Christmas Yet To Come arrives

Scrooge doesn't have to wait for the third ghost to appear, suggesting that the terrible future it predicts is out of his control if he does not make the effort to change. The stave continues the serious tone which began at the end of the previous stave with the description of Ignorance and Want. Dickens slows the pace of the story to ensure the reader listens to his message about the consequences of selfishness. Scrooge is terrified of the Ghost of Christmas Yet To Come because he is afraid of the future, but he knows that the purpose of the ghost's visits is to help him change, so he resolves 'to treasure up every word' from the scenes this ghost will show him.

Scrooge sees what selfishness does to relationships

The ghost takes Scrooge to the 'Change, The Royal Exchange* in London where business deals were conducted and where Scrooge was a frequent visitor. The men, whom Scrooge knew so well because they were so important in business, only care about what will happen to the money belonging to a man who has died and whether there will be a free lunch at the funeral. Scrooge sees 'no likeness of himself', so he doesn't understand why he isn't in his usual place at The Exchange but the reader knows that the dead man being discussed is Scrooge. Dickens therefore is using dramatic irony* which creates tension throughout the stave as the reader watches as Scrooge slowly realises the truth.

Dickens presents poverty in its worst form in this stave when Scrooge and the ghost visit a part of London that 'reeked with crime, with filth and misery'. This shows the reader that in some areas of the city people turn to crime in desperation. The pacey, good-humoured dialogue* between the three criminals who are trading the dead man's possessions shows their cruel attitude and complete disrespect for the man, but it is only because he was so selfish and heartless towards them. They feel no remorse for stealing his bed-curtains, blankets and other personal possessions while he lay there dead on his bed. The ghost aims to shock Scrooge so that when he realises the dead man is him he will be even more likely to want to change his ways.

When the ghost shows Scrooge the dead body of the unknown man under a cover so that his identity is not revealed, it is 'plundered and bereft, unwatched, unwept, uncared for'. Dickens uses emotive language to emphasise the loneliness and isolation of the man. The scene epitomises* the consequences of being isolated from society and focusing solely on wealth rather than building relationships with people.

Scrooge begs to see someone who actually cares about the man's death, so the ghost shows him a family who owe the dead man money and are living in debt but are so frightened because he is '"so merciless a creditor"'. Dickens uses an oxymoron* to show how the father feels a 'serious delight' when he discovers the man has died. The father knows he should not be so delighted because of the man's death but he is happy because his family can now find a more sympathetic money lender. The only positive response to the death is one of relief that the man is dead.

Tiny Tim is mourned and missed

When Scrooge asks to see a more caring response to a death, the ghost shows him the Cratchit family after Tiny Tim has died. The simile* 'the noisy Cratchits were as still as statues in one corner' contrasts with the boisterous, joyful atmosphere on Christmas Day, showing how much the little boy's death has affected the family. Tiny Tim is buried in a 'green' place which is beautiful and contrasts directly with the uncared for place where Scrooge's gravestone is, which is 'walled in by houses and overrun by grass and weeds'. This represents how Tiny Tim was cared for and loved and how little Scrooge meant to anyone when he was alive. Fred's kindness towards the Cratchits in response to Tiny Tim's death also shows that someone apart from his family cared about him, whereas no one at all mourned the dead man. Through this contrast, the reader recognises that it is the poor Tiny Tim who was the happiest in life, not the rich dead man.

Scrooge realises the truth

The dramatic irony* ends as Scrooge recognises that the dead man is him in the future if he does not change his ways. The story then reaches a tense climax* when the ghost shows Scrooge the gravestone bearing his name, so he begs the ghost to tell him that he '"may sponge away the writing on this stone"' and change the future. Dickens continues to build suspense at the end of the stave when Scrooge panics about whether he will have the chance to redeem himself, as he holds his hands 'in a last prayer to have his fate reversed'. By ending the stave on a cliffhanger*, Dickens ensures that the reader wants to find out whether Scrooge is given the opportunity to fulfil his promise and whether he will choose to make amends for his selfish ways. It also gives the Victorian reader time to reflect on their own actions towards the poor in their communities and whether they have time to change themselves.

Stave Five – Scrooge celebrates Christmas and redeems himself

Scrooge is ecstatic to discover that it is Christmas Day and that he still has time to make amends. He buys the biggest turkey in the bakers and pays a boy generously to take it in a cab to the Cratchit family, without them knowing it was him who sent it. Scrooge promises a large sum of money to the charity collector and then joins Fred's family to celebrate Christmas, and Fred welcomes him gladly. Next, Scrooge decides to give Bob Cratchit a pay rise and promises to keep the office warm. He becomes a father figure to Tiny Tim, who has not died, and promises to celebrate Christmas every year and to change his ways all year round. The narrator tells us that in the future Scrooge continues being kind, charitable and always celebrates Christmas. His transformation is complete, and therefore the story has a happy ending.

Analysis

Scrooge is happy and joyful

At the beginning of the final stave, Dickens uses the superlatives* 'best and happiest' to show the great extent to which Scrooge is delighted to find he has the opportunity to 'make amends' for his previous words and actions. He is 'frisking' around the room and laughs a 'splendid laugh', conveying how happy he is; his behaviour is the complete opposite of his cold-hearted attitude in Stave One. Dickens uses this direct contrast to show Scrooge's full transformation to a positive, happy person.

Dickens uses the sense of sound to reinforce the jolly atmosphere, as the church bells are 'ringing out the lustiest peals', with the superlative 'lustiest' emphasising that Scrooge is the happiest he has ever been. This also contrasts with when the church bell tolls in a solemn, sinister manner to signal the arrival of the ghosts. When Scrooge looks outside, there is 'no fog, no mist; clear, bright, jovial, stirring, cold… golden sunlight; Heavenly sky; sweet fresh air'. Dickens' use of pathetic fallacy* contrasts with the thick fog earlier in the novella and represents how

Scrooge now has a clear, enlightened* attitude towards helping those in poverty. It is as if the fog of selfishness has been lifted from Scrooge, as well as from London.

Scrooge is a changed man

Scrooge sends the biggest turkey in the bakery to the Cratchits and uses a series of imperatives* to instruct a young boy to "'Go and buy it'" and "'come back'", showing his determination to do something to help his poor employee and his family. Scrooge says: "'He shan't know who sends it,'" showing that he doesn't want recognition for his kindness. This conveys how he has changed because he is happy to do something for someone else without expecting anyone to give him credit for it. Similarly, when Scrooge makes a large donation to one of the charity collectors whom he sent away earlier in the novella, he doesn't want any thanks or recognition. When the man begins to exclaim how generous Scrooge is, he says: "'Don't say anything, please,'" because he knows how important it is to donate money to support others and not expect to be praised for his kindness.

Scrooge tells Bob to "'make up the fires and buy another coal scuttle'", showing he plans to be a more generous employer in future, who ensures good working conditions in his office. Scrooge has learnt that treating his employee well is the right way to behave. He also tells Bob "'I'll raise your salary'" as he recognises that before he was focused on making as much profit as he could for himself, however now he knows that his employee's happiness and comfort is far more important. When Bob arrives late for work, Scrooge decides to play a joke on him and pretend he is angry when he says: "'What do you mean by coming here at this time of day?'" Scrooge has changed from being strict and serious to fun and humorous.

Scrooge has learnt that the Christmas spirit is important as it makes people happy and inspires them to be kind and generous. He is friendly and polite as he talks to people as he walks around the city on Christmas morning. He 'patted children on the head, and questioned beggars', demonstrating he is now full of the Christmas spirit.

Scrooge becomes part of two families

On Christmas Day, Scrooge accepts Fred's invitation to join his family for their celebrations. He is nervous about how Fred will react after he has been so rude to him in the past and asks "'Will you let me in, Fred?'" Literally he would like Fred to let him enter the house, but metaphorically* he is asking Fred to let him in emotionally and to form a relationship. This shows that Scrooge has learnt the value of family. Similarly, Scrooge tells Bob he will "'endeavour to assist [his] struggling family'" showing that he now has a sense of social responsibility* towards the poor. Not only that but he also becomes a 'second father' to Tiny Tim so that he becomes part of another family too. By joining these two families, Scrooge gains the family that he never had the chance to have because he was so selfish and focused on money. The final words of the novella, 'God bless Us, Every One!', with their religious theme create a festive tone. Dickens wants his readers to feel full of the Christmas spirit but to act on his key message, which is to be more generous towards those in poverty and to be kind at Christmas time and all year round.

Progress and revision check

1. On what day of the year does the story begin?

2. Where was the young Scrooge left alone at Christmas time?

3. What are the names of the two children that the Ghost of Christmas Present reveals from under his robes?

4. What are the occupations of the three people who sell the dead man's possessions?

5. What does Scrooge send in a cab to the Cratchits on Christmas Day?

6. What does the 'fog and darkness' represent at the beginning of the story?

7. Why does Scrooge try to hide the light that is shining from the Ghost of Christmas Past?

8. Why does Dickens juxtapose* the Christmas celebrations with the description of the children Ignorance and Want?

9. What is the effect of the use of dramatic irony* when the reader knows who the dead man is but Scrooge hasn't realised yet?

10. What does the use of pathetic fallacy represent in the final stave?

~ Characters ~

Major characters

Ebenezer Scrooge

Stave One

Scrooge is cold-hearted and isolated

Dickens introduces Scrooge as 'hard and sharp as flint', using a simile* to compare him to a small piece of solid rock to show how unfeeling and uncaring he is. Dickens suggests that Scrooge has such a tough exterior that he does not let anyone get close to him and his words are so cruel and harsh that they are sharp and have the potential to emotionally hurt or offend people. Dickens also uses freezing imagery when he says Scrooge 'carried his own low temperature always' to convey how he is cold-hearted and unfriendly towards other people. Scrooge is therefore not someone who others want to socialise with, and similarly he does not want to be a part of society anyway, as he warns 'all human sympathy to keep its distance'. Scrooge would rather keep people away from him than talk to them or form any relationship. Dickens immediately sets Scrooge up as an unlikeable character from the beginning.

Scrooge doesn't care about poverty

Scrooge doesn't believe in helping those living in poverty and he feels it is the government's responsibility to support them. When the charity collectors visit Scrooge to ask for money he says: '"Are there no prisons?"' and '"The Treadmill* and the Poor Law* are in full vigour then?"'. Scrooge believes that the government already provide somewhere for poor people to live and work and so he should not have to give them extra support. Even though is it likely he is aware of the terrible conditions in the workhouses*, he doesn't feel it is his responsibility to help the people who work there, which makes his uncaring attitude even more shocking. Scrooge cares more about his own wealth and profit and does not want to be charitable, saying "'It's enough for a man to understand his own business'". This shows that Scrooge's priority is to look after himself.

Marley's ghost affects Scrooge

Scrooge's fear of Marley's ghost is evident from the very beginning. He tries to convince himself that his vision of Marley's ghost is a result of something he has eaten which is making him see things that aren't really there. By the end of the stave we begin to see a change in Scrooge's attitude as he speaks to Marley's ghost 'with humility and deference'. He also 'began to quake exceedingly' which suggests the ghost's warning has affected him so much that he is shaking. Scrooge has been made aware that he is living a selfish life and that there are consequences for his actions, which prompts him to consider his current behaviour. Dickens introduces Scrooge as cold and harsh so that we believe he may not be capable of change, but as he is afraid of Marley's ghost we see a hint that there could be a part of him that knows that the way he lives his life is not the best way to be.

Stave Two

Scrooge is emotional about his childhood

Dickens shows the reader an emotional response from the usually cold-hearted Scrooge when the ghost shows him 'a solitary* child, neglected by his friends,' at school at Christmas time. Scrooge sobs, conveying his sad emotional response to his isolation as a child, which makes the reader feel sorry for him for the first time. We can see that he was lonely and now feels sad about it, so possibly he is still upset by his loneliness as an adult and doesn't necessarily want to be this way. This suggests that Scrooge may want to change and become more sociable and part of society, hinting at his possible transformation later in the story. Scrooge is beginning to learn to feel pity and empathy* again as 'with a rapidity of transition very foreign to his usual character' he feels pity for himself as a child. This leads the reader to believe that Scrooge has the potential to feel this way towards others too.

Scrooge had good relationships

Dickens shows us that Scrooge had a close relationship with his sister Fan, whom he calls '"quite a woman"'. We see how he was once capable of affection but the loss of such an important person in his life helps to explain why Scrooge pushes people away – it could be that he doesn't want to risk losing someone again and feeling the pain of loss. Through Fan, Dickens foreshadows* Scrooge's change as we can see that he may be capable of being kind, caring and loving again. We see Scrooge begin to change his attitude towards his family as he feels 'uneasy in his mind' when the ghost reminds him that Fred is Fan's son. Scrooge realises that he has not valued the family he still has.

As an apprentice for Mr Fezziwig, Scrooge was lively and animated as he 'came briskly in' to the room, ready to celebrate at his boss' Christmas party. This contrasts with Scrooge now and shows how he was once youthful and full of positivity. As he observes the party, Scrooge begins to understand the value of happiness when he praises Mr Fezziwig's generosity towards his employees, whom he says '"has the power to render us happy or unhappy"'. This makes him regret how he has treated Bob Cratchit, and he says he "'should like to be able to say a word or two to my clerk just now'" because he realises he needs to be a kinder and more generous employer.

Dickens also shows how Scrooge was a kinder, more affectionate person when he was in a loving relationship with Belle. However, she tells him "'You are changed'", conveying how he became more selfish and greedy when he focused on money. When Scrooge sees Belle with her family, he regrets not having children of his own and 'his sight grew very dim indeed'. Dickens uses this image of his sight to suggest that Scrooge realises how dark and lonely his life has been without a family of his own and that he should make more of an effort to be part of other people's lives.

Stave Three and Four

Scrooge learns from the Ghosts

While Scrooge waits for the Ghost of Christmas Present's arrival in Stave Three he suffers 'a violent fit of trembling'. He is afraid of what the ghost may show him which indicates that he is taking the ghosts' lessons seriously and he knows that the consequences of not listening to them could be terrible for him and for others. Similarly, Scrooge is frightened of the Ghost of Christmas Yet To Come in Stave Four, as when it moves towards him, it 'filled him with a solemn dread'. He knows that the ghost will show him the future and he is terrified about what it will hold for him. However, he is now more willing to learn from the spirits, as he says "'I hope to be another man from what I was'". Scrooge recognises that the ghosts are there to help him and that he needs to follow their advice in order to become a better person.

Scrooge's attitude to poverty changes

Scrooge shows that he cares about what will happen to Tiny Tim when he asks the ghost with interest: "'tell me if Tiny Tim will live'". To remind Scrooge of his previous uncaring attitude towards those in poverty like Tiny Tim, the ghost repeats his words that the 'surplus population' should be reduced through allowing poor people to die. This causes Scrooge to be 'overcome with penitence and grief', which shows he feels remorseful. Because he feels ashamed we know that he recognises that he needs to change. As they leave the Cratchits', Scrooge is watching Tiny Tim carefully, which confirms that he is changing as he cares about the fate of someone else in the future and not just about what will happen to himself. The reader begins to learn here that he is not changing just to help himself, but to help others also.

Scrooge learns how others see him

In Stave Three, when Mrs Cratchit describes Scrooge as an "'odious, stingy, hard, unfeeling, man'", we see how strongly she feels about the way he treats his employee, her husband, as she uses a list of negative adjectives* to describe how much she detests him. This allows Scrooge to see how someone else sees him as a result of his focus on money rather than the welfare of his employee. When the ghost and Scrooge observe Fred's Christmas celebrations, Fred says Scrooge is "'not so pleasant as he might be'", while Fred's wife says "'I have no patience with him'". Scrooge is able to see other people's negative views of him because of his selfish and miserly* attitude and this prompts him to want to be seen more positively.

Similarly, in Stave Four when the ghost shows Scrooge the businessmen at The Exchange*, they refer to him as "'Old Scratch*'".

Even those who held the same values of profit and wealth as Scrooge saw him as an evil, devilish character, showing he was unpopular even with those who appear to be similar to him. The fact that the businessmen, who appear unkind and selfish, refer to Scrooge as the devil shows that he must be even worse than them. Also in Stave Four, Scrooge's charwoman* calls him a '"wicked old screw"', highlighting his cruelty and meanness, and she says he would not have been so lonely when he died if he had not been so cruel when he was alive. Finally, the father of the young family who owed Scrooge money says they would be unlucky to have '"so merciless a creditor"' as Scrooge in future, highlighting Scrooge's lack of sympathy for their poverty. Again this allows Scrooge to see how others view his behaviour and therefore makes him think more seriously about the way he has been living his life and the effect his behaviour has on others. The fact that he now cares what other people think of him shows that he is beginning to change.

Scrooge begins to enjoy Christmas

As Scrooge observes Fred's family party, we can see that he is changing as he 'softened more and more', as he enjoys listening to the Christmas music. Whereas before Scrooge hated anything to do with Christmas, he is now beginning to see the value of Christmas traditions and the happiness that they bring, even though they don't create a profit or wealth. As Scrooge and the ghost watch the games at the party, Scrooge 'begged like a boy to be allowed to stay until the guests departed'. His childlike attitude suggests that he has rediscovered fun and excitement and how they make him feel positive and happy. He is aware that it is being with others that creates this feeling, so he is eager to be around his family again and form relationships once more. He becomes 'so gay and light of heart' when Fred toasts him, signalling a clear change from the miserly, negative person he once was.

Stave Five

Scrooge is redeemed

Scrooge uses a series of similes to express his happiness at being given the chance to redeem himself, including "'I am as light as a feather'". This suggests that the heavy burden of sad memories that he has been carrying around for most of his life has been lifted. He knows that by being more generous and kind he will be a happier person, which means he will no longer be weighed down by his misery.

Dickens uses personification* to describe Scrooge's laugh as 'the father of a long, long line of laughs!'. This suggests there will metaphorically* be many generations of laughs to come in the future. Before this, Scrooge didn't laugh or embrace humour at all, but this use of personification suggests that he is committed to being a positive, happy person and it is not just a temporary change in behaviour: he will adopt this attitude for the rest of his life, showing his complete transformation.

Scrooge values generosity, charity and family

The final stave confirms that Scrooge's attitude has changed as he sends the Cratchits a large turkey, conveying how he understands the importance of being generous towards others. When he meets one of the charity collectors whom he refused to give money to, it 'sent a pang across his heart' because he feels so ashamed for rejecting their requests when they wanted to help those less fortunate in society. Scrooge feels nervous when he realises how badly he has behaved towards his nephew Fred by rejecting his hospitality because 'he passed the door a dozen times, before he had the courage to go up and knock'. This shows that he wants his family to accept him because he has made the decision to be part of their lives and he doesn't want to be rejected now that he knows how important family is.

Scrooge appreciates Christmas

In contrast to Stave One, the narrator says that Scrooge 'became as good a friend, as good a master, and as good a man, as the old city knew'. The repetition of the adjective* 'good' emphasises how he is a changed man who cares about his role in society and the effect he can have on others. The novella ends with the narrator telling us that Scrooge 'knew how to keep Christmas well', showing how his attitude towards Christmas has changed and that he recognises that Christmas values such as charity, kindness and forgiveness are important for helping everyone in society.

Jacob Marley

Marley's appearance

Dickens presents Marley's ghost as sinister and frightening so that Scrooge is scared of his appearance and is more likely to listen to the lessons it has to teach him. The ghost aims to shock Scrooge into believing he really has returned when he takes the bandage off his head and his 'lower jaw dropped down upon its breast!'. Even though he is a ghost, Scrooge must believe that Marley's ghost is real so that he doesn't think he is just part of his imagination. He must understand that Marley's ghost has a purpose and has come to warn him that he must change his selfish ways. In Victorian times, dead bodies had their jaws bandaged so they would stay together as they no longer had the muscle strength to keep them closed. Marley appears like a realistic deathly corpse to prove to Scrooge that he has been dead for seven years and to convince Scrooge that the message he brings is serious.

Similarly, Dickens aims to shock the reader so that they will take notice when the ghost expresses his remorse for being so selfish and greedy when he was alive. When he looks at the ghost, Scrooge 'felt the chilling influence of its death-cold eyes' and its voice 'disturbed the very marrow of his bones', showing that Scrooge is petrified of the ghost as when he last saw Marley seven years ago he was a living, breathing friend. Dickens uses cold imagery such as 'death-cold' and 'chilling' to convey how Marley's ghost epitomises* death and causes Scrooge to feel thoroughly anxious due to the ghost's unexpected, disturbing arrival.

Marley feels guilt and remorse

Marley uses dramatic and serious vocabulary to show how deeply he has been affected by his selfish actions when he was alive, saying he is 'doomed to wander through the world – oh woe is me! – and witness what it cannot share, but might have shared on earth, and turned to happiness!'. Marley's ghost must roam the world watching the suffering of the people he would have been able to help when he was alive and chose not to. Marley admits that it was his choice to focus on profit and money when he was alive, so he takes responsibility for neglecting to care for other people when he says: "'I girded it on of my own free will, and of my own free will I wore it"'. Marley's reference to the idea of 'free will' suggests that Scrooge also has the option to be more charitable and kind, he has just chosen not to be. Dickens suggests that everyone in society has the chance to help others if only they make the decision to be more thoughtful about those less fortunate than themselves.

Marley's ghost warns Scrooge

Towards the end of the stave, Marley's ghost seems to become increasingly agitated as it 'clanked its chain so hideously in the dead silence of the night'. The contrast between the loud sound 'clanked' and the 'dead silence' helps to create a sinister atmosphere and emphasises how Marley's ghost is desperate for Scrooge to understand his message if he is to have any chance of redeeming himself. This agitation increases the dramatic tension and the pace of the story, suggesting his time with Scrooge is running out and how it is urgent that Scrooge begins learning from the next three ghosts as soon as possible.

Before he leaves, Marley explicitly states why he has come to visit Scrooge – to help him change: "'I am here tonight to warn you, that you have yet a chance and hope of escaping my fate'". Marley wants to show Scrooge how serious the consequences are if he does not become more caring and charitable while he is alive. By appearing so remorseful about his actions and wanting to support Scrooge, we can see that Marley is capable of change. So Dickens hints that Scrooge, whose current attitude is the same as Marley's once was, also has the potential to change. Marley's ghost serves to warn Scrooge, and the readers, of what could happen if they choose not to change.

Fred

Fred's appearance and personality

Dickens introduces Fred as a foil* to Scrooge in order to show a contrast between the two characters and to emphasise how selfish and miserable Scrooge is. When Fred enters Scrooge's office he is 'all in a glow; his face was ruddy and handsome; his eyes sparkled' showing that he has a cheerful, friendly and warm personality. This description is the opposite of the cold imagery that Dickens uses to convey Scrooge's uncaring, cold-hearted nature. Fred's laughter is referred to throughout the novella to show he is positive and optimistic which again contrasts to the pessimistic Scrooge who only sees benefits from business and making money.

Fred values Christmas

Fred sees Christmas as worth celebrating, even though Scrooge disagrees because he doesn't make any money from it. Fred believes that even though Christmas hasn't improved his financial situation, there are other ways that he has benefitted from it which are worth much more to him, such as the happiness it brings and family celebrations. He says "'it has done me good and will do me good'", suggesting that every year he has gained something from Christmas and so he intends to continue to celebrate the festive season, even if Scrooge continues to hate Christmas, be rude to him and to reject his requests to join his family on Christmas Day.

Dickens also uses Fred to represent the wealthy people in society who co care about those living in poverty. Fred believes that Christmas is a time to support the poor, as he says it is "'a good time: a kind, forgiving, charitable, pleasant time'". Dickens uses Fred to convey his own attitude that the rich should support the poor at Christmas time and all year round. By presenting Fred as a likeable and friendly character who has good moral values, Dickens prompts the reader to question whether they could be more like Fred and they are more likely to want to live their life the way Fred does.

Fred values family

Unlike Scrooge, family is important to Fred, which is clear when he insists that Scrooge joins his family's Christmas celebrations: "'Don't be angry, uncle. Come! Dine with us tomorrow!'" Fred's use of the imperative verbs* 'come' and 'dine' suggests he is determined to encourage Scrooge to be part of the family. He also uses the affectionate family term 'uncle', suggesting that he will not give up on Scrooge because he is someone whom his mother, Scrooge's sister, had a close relationship with. Similarly, Fred later tells his family how he will continue to include Scrooge when he says: "'I mean to give him the same chance every year, whether he likes it or not, for I pity him'". Fred thinks it is important to be with family at Christmas time and to give them the opportunity to redeem themselves. This reminds the readers of Fan, Fred's mother, who was also determined to include Scrooge at Christmas, showing that they both value family, unlike Scrooge.

Fred sees the good in Scrooge

Fred continues to forgive Scrooge for being rude to him and will not say a bad word about him as he knows Scrooge is already suffering by isolating himself from his family. Fred says "'his offences carry their own punishment, and I have nothing to say against him'". He knows that because Scrooge is not taking advantage of all the benefits that being full of the Christmas spirit brings, such as happiness, kindness and being with family, Scrooge is missing out so there is no need for him to be angry at him. Fred is so self-assured and confident with his own choices in life that he doesn't take Scrooge's rejection personally and is not upset by his attitude.

Despite his regular rejections, Fred welcomes Scrooge enthusiastically when he unexpectedly arrives to celebrate Christmas with him and his family. When the narrator explains how it was 'a mercy he didn't shake his arm off', we see how pleased Fred is that his uncle has changed his mind and wants to be part of the family. Fred doesn't question why Scrooge has changed his mind or ask him what happened to make him want to celebrate Christmas, or even mock him for his previous attitude. He just accepts Scrooge's decision without asking any questions. Dickens choses to portray Fred as cheerful, charitable and forgiving so that the reader wants to become someone like him who is kind and helps those in poverty.

The Cratchits

The Cratchits are a poor but happy family

Dickens uses the Cratchits to represent Victorian families living in poverty. Although they are not as poor as those living in extreme poverty, Dickens wants to show all levels of need, including those who do work but still have little money. The Cratchits are 'not well dressed; their shoes were far from being water-proof; their clothes were scanty', which reinforces their lack of money. However, despite being poor, the Cratchits are 'happy, grateful, pleased with one another, and contented with the time'. Dickens wants to show that family is more important than money to the Cratchits and he uses them as a contrast to the lonely, greedy Scrooge.

Tiny Tim

Tiny Tim is physically disabled and needs support for his weak, fragile little body. He has a 'little crutch' and his legs are 'supported by an iron frame'. Although Dickens never specifically tells us what is wrong with Tiny Tim and why he will die if Scrooge does not change and become more generous towards the poor, the suggestion is that he suffers from a condition that he could recover from if he had better living conditions and health as a result of having more money. Tiny Tim is therefore a key figure in the novella as he prompts Scrooge to see how he needs to change his unsympathetic attitude towards the poor. This sets Scrooge on the path to redemption* and leads to his transformation to becoming a better person.

Despite his disability, Tiny Tim makes the most of his life and joins in with the family merriment at Christmas dinner when he beats on the table with 'the handle of his knife'. He also attends church with his father, Bob, and believes that his condition will help others to strengthen their Christian faith. He 'hoped the people saw him in the church, because he was a cripple' so they would remember the miracles Jesus performed when he 'made lame* beggars walk and blind men see'. Tiny Tim wants people to think that Jesus is responsible for him being alive and so they will be confident in their faith that he is looking after them and helps the poor and disabled.

In Victorian times, the disabled child who is disadvantaged by their disability but accepts their condition was a common character in literature and, in A Christmas Carol, Tiny Tim fulfils this role. Dickens uses Tiny Tim to represent the reality behind the 'surplus population' that Scrooge believes should die in order to solve the social problem of poverty. He aims to provoke sympathy in the reader so that they want to become more generous to help children like Tiny Tim.

Bob Cratchit is close to his children

Bob is a good father and has a close relationship with his children. He carries Tiny Tim 'upon his shoulder' showing how he physically supports him because he is frail and ill but also how he metaphorically supports and guides him as his father. Bob is also close to his daughter Martha and he is disappointed when the family pretend she will not be joining them for Christmas. When she appears, Bob 'hugged his daughter to his heart's content', showing that all of his family being together on Christmas Day is very important to him. Bob is very proud of Tiny Tim because of the way he accepts his disability gracefully and has a positive attitude to life. However, his worry and anxiety is evident when Dickens describes his voice as 'tremulous' as it shows how concerned he is about what will happen to Tiny Tim. His voice trembles because he knows that many children who are ill do not survive childhood and that there are few opportunities for disabled children to find employment and earn a living, so Tiny Tim does not have the same chance to escape poverty as his siblings.

Mrs Cratchit is a loving mother

Mrs Cratchit's dress is old but she has made an effort to make it look special for Christmas. She and her daughter Belinda are described as 'brave in ribbons' conveying how they are determined not to let being poor get in the way of presenting themselves nicely for a special occasion. Mrs Cratchit is a caring, resourceful mother who, despite their lack of money, does her best to provide enough food for her family at Christmas. The dinner has to be 'eked out by the apple-sauce and mashed potatoes', suggesting there is not enough quality food for the whole family. However, none of them complain or show their disappointment which shows their respect for their mother's efforts and their appreciation that they are together as a family.

The Cratchit children work hard

Peter is ambitious and willing to work hard. He is proud that he may one day become 'a man of business' showing that he has high aspirations despite his background. Martha is a 'poor apprentice at a milliner's*' which was a more respectable role than working in a factory, but she still has to work long hours, even at Christmas. She is also a hard worker as she tells her family 'how many hours she worked at a stretch'. Dickens uses the Cratchit children to emphasise that the lower classes were not lazy, which is what many of the higher classes believed. The younger Cratchit children do not work yet but make their home lively and chaotic. They 'danced about the table,' creating a cheerful, positive atmosphere despite their poverty.

The Ghost of Christmas Past

The ghost's appearance

The purpose of the Ghost of Christmas Past is to remind Scrooge of the person he once was when he was young and to help him think about how he has changed and become more miserly* and selfish. Dickens uses personification to represent Scrooge's life through the ghost when he describes its appearance as 'like a child; yet not so like a child as an old man'. This suggests that the ghost will show Scrooge scenes from his youth and how they have influenced the old man he has become. Similarly, Dickens uses symbolism* when he says the ghost 'held a branch of fresh green holly' and its dress is 'trimmed with summer flowers'. The summer flowers represent Scrooge as a child and the memories from his youth, while the holly represents winter and therefore the later years in his life.

The changes in the ghost's appearance, which is 'light one instant, at another time was dark', represent how it will show Scrooge both happy and sad memories from his past to help him understand why he has become so isolated and selfish. This change between light and dark could also show how, when Scrooge was younger, his life was bright and cheerful but, now that he focuses on money and profit, it has become dark and lonely. Dickens aims to provoke sympathy for Scrooge from the reader as they can see that he was once happy. However, the pain that his family life, school life and his relationships caused him have resulted in his isolation and unhappiness.

The way the ghost speaks

The ghost's voice represents Scrooge's past as it is 'soft and gentle' and as if it were 'at a distance'. The past, when Scrooge was kinder and happier, is far away from his present life but it still there in the background, reminding him that if he wants to, he can change. However, the ghost is also firm and uses imperative verbs* to instruct Scrooge: '"Rise! and walk with me!"' so that Scrooge knows it is serious about the lessons it has to teach him. The ghost also asks Scrooge questions to help him think about how he might change, such as '"What is the matter?"'. He wants Scrooge to think about the answers for himself and not have to tell him how he can become a better person. Dickens uses the Ghost of Christmas Past to remind Scrooge of the happy, positive person he once was and to prompt him to think about how he can take his first steps towards his redemption and become a better person.

The Ghost of Christmas Present

The ghost's appearance

The purpose of the Ghost of Christmas Present is to show Scrooge how other people celebrate Christmas, even those with very little money. The ghost is introduced as 'a jolly Giant,' with 'sparkling eye… cheery voice…joyful air!'. This cheerful, happy personality emphasises how Christmas is a time for positivity and celebration. The ghost is also friendly and welcoming towards Scrooge when it says '"Come in! and know me better, man!"'. This gives the impression that the ghost is pleased to see Scrooge and wants to help him change his ways.

Dickens uses a reference to classical mythology when he describes the ghost as holding 'a glowing torch' shaped like 'Plenty's horn'. In the mythological stories 'Plenty's horn' is a symbol* of abundance* and nourishment, so here it represents how at Christmas time there is lots of food, therefore Dickens argues that there is plenty of food for everyone. He criticises Thomas Malthus' view that the poor should die to control the population because there is not enough food to go around. The torch is used by the ghost to spread happiness at Christmas time and to stop people arguing, showing how Christmas should be a time for forgiveness and goodwill. Dickens also uses a symbol as the ghost wears a sheath without a sword which is 'eaten up with rust' showing how Christmas is a time of peace. The 'rust' suggests that the sheath has not been used for a long time and the sword has long since gone, representing that there should be no conflict or fighting at Christmas.

The ghost cares about the poor

Dickens shows how the ghost cares about those living in poverty, as it has 'sympathy with all poor men'. Through the ghost, Dickens conveys now he believes that Christmas should be a time of thinking about those less fortunate. The ghost also aims to awaken Scrooge to the reality of the consequences of his selfish attitude towards poverty by showing him Tiny Tim and saying: "'If these shadows remain unaltered by the Future, the child will die'". The ghost wants to shock Scrooge into seeing how an innocent, vulnerable child can be directly affected by the selfish attitude of those who have plenty of money but keep it for themselves.

Dickens personifies the causes of poverty through the girl and boy, Ignorance and Want, who are hiding under the ghost's robes. While the ghost appears happy and jolly, Dickens shows how Christmas hides the reality of poverty and he uses the innocent children to shock and upset both Scrooge and the reader. Through the ghost, Dickens warns that unless society changes and looks after the poor then everyone will suffer. The fact that they are children also suggests that this problem will continue for generations if it is not solved. When the ghost says about Ignorance, "'beware this boy'", he conveys how a lack of education is the main reason for poverty and how having knowledge is the most important way to help people out of their situation. The ghost says society will face 'doom' if many people are uneducated and poor.

The Ghost of Christmas Yet To Come

The ghost's appearance

The purpose of the Ghost of Christmas Yet To Come is to show Scrooge what will happen if he does not change his selfish ways. It aims to frighten him so that he will want to become a more generous, caring person. Dickens introduces the third ghost as 'a solemn phantom*, draped and hooded, coming, like a mist along the ground', towards Scrooge. He uses a simile* to compare the ghost to low mist so that it

A Christmas Carol: Revision Guide for GCSE

seems like it is slowly gliding along, threatening to make Scrooge feel confused and afraid. Unlike the Ghost of Christmas Present, who sprinkles happiness with his torch, the Ghost of Christmas Yet To Come 'seemed to scatter gloom and mystery', suggesting that if Scrooge does not listen to the lessons it teaches then the consequences are very serious for both him and society.

A Victorian reader would recognise the ghost as personifying death, as it looks like the Grim Reaper; it is 'shrouded in a deep black garment, which concealed its head, its face, its form'. This foreshadows* a death, which makes Scrooge and the reader terrified about what the ghost is going to reveal. Dickens also presents the ghost's face as hidden in order to convey how we cannot see the future and that the only certainty in life is death.

The ghost's actions

The ghost frightens Scrooge, as he 'feared the silent shape so much that his legs trembled beneath him'. This shows how he is afraid of the future that the ghost is about to show him and what the consequences of his selfish behaviour will be.

The ghost is silent and only communicates through actions because it wants Scrooge to take control of his decisions and draw his own conclusions about what he must do to change the future. This gives Scrooge more responsibility for the change in his behaviour and ensures that it is genuine, rather than if he just did what the ghost told him to do.

The ghost has a very quick pace when it is showing Scrooge the future, as it 'did not stay for anything'. It wants to give Scrooge a sense of

~ Characters ~   55 urgency and push him to change quickly because the serious, negative consequences of his current behaviour will happen soon if he doesn't.

The ghost cares about Scrooge

Although the ghost appears frightening and sinister, towards the end of the stave we see its more sympathetic side when its 'hand appeared to shake' and its 'kind hand trembled'. This suggests that the ghost is emotional about Scrooge's journey towards redemption and it wants to help him change. The ghost appears to genuinely care about what will happen to him but we can see why it was necessary for it to appear so frightening because it is so important that Scrooge sees the error of his ways. Dickens presents the ghost as sinister to possibly scare his Victorian readers, some of whom were superstitious, so that they may also want to change.

Minor characters

Fan

Dickens uses the character of Fan to show us that Scrooge was once a loving person and that someone loved him in return. As a girl, Fan is a lively character who is 'brimful of glee' because she is so happy that she has arrived at Scrooge's school to bring him home for Christmas. The language the siblings use shows the reader that they had a close relationship; Fan uses the repetition of the affectionate term 'dear' when she calls Scrooge: '"Dear, dear brother"' and he says to her: '"You are quite a woman, little Fan!"' expressing his admiration that she has organised to be with him at Christmas time.

Fan was Fred's mother and we can see the similarities between them. Fan is determined to change their father's mind and let Scrooge come home from school for Christmas when she says: "'I was not afraid to ask him more than once if you might come home'". Similarly, Fred wants to persuade Scrooge to spend Christmas Day with his family, showing that they both want Scrooge to be part of their families.

However, we discover that Fan has since died, which makes us feel sorry for Scrooge because he has lost someone that he loves. Therefore, we understand that he may be isolating himself from his family because the memory of losing his sister hurts too much and Fred may remind him of his mother, the sister Scrooge has lost.

Mr Fezziwig

Mr Fezziwig, in contrast to Scrooge, is a generous employer: 'fuel was heaped upon the fire; and the warehouse was as snug, and warm, and dry, and bright.' Unlike Scrooge, he keeps his office warm for his employees because he cares about their welfare and believes that he should look after the people who work for him.

At his Christmas party, Mr Fezziwig makes sure everyone has enough to eat and drink. Mr and Mrs Fezziwig clearly value each of their employees as they are all invited to take part in the Christmas celebrations: 'In came the housemaid, with her cousin, the baker. In came the cook, with her brother's particular friend, the milkman.' Dickens uses the repetition of 'In came' to emphasise how many people were at the party and how they are all included, whatever their role or status.

By using a metaphor* to describe Mr Fezziwig's voice as 'comfortable, oily, rich, fat, jovial', Dickens shows how Mr Fezziwig makes those who have less money than him feel full of food, drink and happiness at Christmas time. Similarly, Dickens uses a simile* to describe Mr Fezziwig's dancing: 'A positive light appeared to issue from Fezziwig's calves. They shone in every part of the dance like moons.' This represents how his positivity and generosity lights up every part of the room.

At the end of the party Mr and Mrs Fezziwig stand at their door 'shaking hands with every person individually as he or she went out'. The Fezziwigs treat everyone equally and value them as unique individuals, not just part of a workforce to make them money. Watching the Fezziwigs makes Scrooge want to become a more generous employer and to treat Bob Cratchit the way Mr Fezziwig used to treat him.

Belle

We meet Belle wearing 'mourning-dress' which suggests she has lost her parents and is now poor, so she believes that Scrooge will not want to marry her as she cannot bring any money to the marriage. Belle breaks her engagement with Scrooge because he has become more interested in money than her. She says that an 'idol*' has taken her place and this metaphor represents how money is more important to Scrooge than their relationship. It shows how he worships profit and wealth rather than valuing building a life with her.

When she leaves him, Belle is sure of her decision as she knows Scrooge has made the choice to follow wealth. She says: '"May you be happy in the life you have chosen"', showing that she does care about him but she knows that they don't share the same priorities such as family and relationships. The ghost shows Scrooge that Belle becomes a mother and has a family in the future and is happy, despite being poor.

In contrast, Belle's husband tells his family that he has just seen Scrooge in his office "'quite alone in the world'" because he chose money over love.

Dickens uses the character Belle to emphasise how Scrooge's greed has led to his isolation and solitary* life. However, similar to Fan, Belle shows how Scrooge was once in a loving relationship and was capable of connecting with another human being, so we realise that he does have the potential to change and be more loving.

Ignorance* and Want*

Ignorance and Want are two children who personify poverty in Victorian England. They are not real characters but they symbolise the problems that cause poverty. By naming the children, Dickens suggests that poverty is caused by 'ignorance' which is a lack of knowledge as a result of having no education. Without this knowledge, poor people struggle to get better jobs to earn more money so they can have a better lifestyle. He also says poverty is caused by 'want' which is when poor people need food, shelter and warmth in order to live a healthy life.

Dickens uses a list of shocking adjectives* to describe Ignorance and Want, including 'wretched, abject, frightful, hideous, miserable' and 'yellow, meagre, ragged, scowling, wolfish'. He bombards the reader with a detailed description so that they understand the full impact of poverty on the children. 'Wretched and miserable' show how significantly the children have been affected emotionally, while 'frightful and hideous' convey how they are almost unbearable to look at. Dickens dehumanises* the children through the adjectives 'wolfish' and 'scowling' suggesting that they have become like animals due to lack of nourishment and education.

The Victorians saw children as innocent, so Dickens aims to horrify the reader by showing the impact poverty has had on them. He wants the reader to change their selfish ways so that the issue of poverty is addressed and society as a whole can benefit – ultimately, he believes, it is everyone's responsibility.

Progress and revision check

1. How many years before the novella begins did Marley die?
2. What does the character Tiny Tim represent?
3. What does Fred believe is important at Christmas time?
4. Why does the Ghost of Christmas Past ask Scrooge questions?
5. What does the Ghost of Christmas Present's torch do?
6. Why is the face of the Ghost of Christmas Yet To Come hidden?
7. How are Fred and Fan similar?
8. What are the differences between Mr Fezziwig and Scrooge as employers?
9. Why doesn't Scrooge feel he should be charitable in Stave One?
10. What does Scrooge's generosity show about him in Stave Five?

~ Themes ~

The Christmas Spirit

Happiness

At the beginning of the novella, Scrooge doesn't see the value of the Christmas spirit. He believes that anyone who wishes someone else a "Merry Christmas" is a fool and should be '"boiled with his own pudding"'. His aggressive language shows how bitter he is about the festive season and how strongly he feels that there are no benefits to celebrating it. However, in direct contrast to Scrooge, Fred sees Christmas as a time of happiness and believes '"it has done me good and will do me good"'. Fred will not allow Scrooge and his miserable attitude to stop him from enjoying the celebrations. Dickens uses this contrast to highlight how much impact being full of the Christmas spirit has on the level of happiness someone experiences.

Dickens also presents how, at Christmas time, people are happier than at other times of the year because of the positivity that Christmas brings. Outside they are clearing snow, playing with snowballs and everyone is 'jovial and full of glee' and 'laughing heartily'. Despite their lack of money, the Cratchit family are happy at Christmas because they are celebrating the occasion together; they are 'happy, grateful, pleased with one another, and contented with the time'.

At the end of the novella, Scrooge is transformed and, to highlight this, Dickens shows that he is full of the Christmas spirit, as he gives everyone 'a delighted smile'. This is a complete contrast to the miserable, lonely person he was at the beginning who detested Christmas and anyone who celebrated it. Dickens wants to show how

Scrooge has learnt the value of the Christmas spirit and how it brings happiness in the festive season.

Religion

Dickens describes Christmas as a religious celebration, as many Victorians would see this time of year as a time for celebrating the birth of Christ. He includes many references to Christianity because he feels that the values it teaches, such as charity and forgiveness, are important to uphold at Christmas time and that they contribute to filling someone with the Christmas spirit. Dickens reflects the religious nature of the Victorians and their attendance at church on Christmas Day by describing how people are 'flocking through the streets' to churches and chapels.

The narrator comments on how Christmas games, which can make adults act like children, are appropriate because Jesus was a child on the first Christmas Day: 'it is good to be children sometimes, and never better than at Christmas, when the mighty Founder was a child himself.' Dickens shows that although strict Christians would not approve of parties and games at Christmas time, people should have fun because Jesus himself was once a child and he would think being filled with the Christmas spirit as a result of celebrating was good for people at this time of year.

Tiny Tim is very religious and requests a blessing from God when the family are celebrating and says "'God bless us every one!'". The narrator also uses religious terminology to refer to Tiny Tim and to comment on how he was sent by God to die in order to teach Scrooge to change his ways: 'Spirit of Tiny Tim, thy childish essence was from God!'. In much in the same way, Christians believe that Jesus was sent by God to die in the place of people who have sinned* so that they will be forgiven.

Traditional celebrations

Dickens also presents the secular* side of Christmas and how the Christmas spirit is not only found in religious celebrations but also in time with family and friends. Mr Fezziwig holds a Christmas party for all of his employees, showing that he is full of the Christmas spirit. He makes everyone feel involved and is generous with heating and food: 'fuel was heaped upon the fire; and the warehouse was as snug, and warm, and dry, and bright as a ball-room'. This contrasts starkly with the lack of warmth in Scrooge's office, where the Christmas spirit is not embraced. At Fred's house, he and his family are playing games and listening to music. They are all full of the Christmas spirit because they are celebrating together, which contrasts to the isolated, miserable Scrooge who spends the season alone.

The Ghost of Christmas Present personifies the Christmas spirit. He spreads Christmas cheer with his torch and has a 'kind, generous, hearty nature'. The ghost also appears in a room full of Christmas food and traditional decorations, emphasising how everything about him represents Christmas. He is responsible for spreading the Christmas spirit which inspires people to be forgiving and kind.

Charity

Fred voices Dickens' views that Christmas should be a time for giving, when he says that everyone should '"think of people below them as if they really were fellow passengers to the grave"'. This highlights Dickens' opinion that people with a lot of money should support those in poverty, as the poor are still people just like them and ultimately everyone dies, whatever level of affluence* they are born with. The charity collectors also believe that Christmas is a time for giving. They are full of the generous Christmas spirit when they say that they choose to help at Christmas because it is a time when '"Want is keenly felt and Abundance* rejoices"'. The charity collectors know that at Christmas time in particular there are many people living in poverty as well as many people with far more food and gifts than they need, so they believe that the wealthy should share what they have with those less fortunate.

Dickens intentionally uses the Ghost of Christmas Present to reveal the children Ignorance and Want who are 'wretched, abject, frightful, hideous, miserable'. The ghost represents the joyful side of Christmas but Dickens conveys the idea that behind this is the poverty and misery that needs to be supported through charity at this time of year. By the end of the novella, Scrooge has learnt the importance of being generous towards others. He buys the Cratchits a large turkey and gives a substantial amount of money to one of the charity collectors, with '"many back-payments"'. Scrooge has learnt that being charitable benefits everyone and leads to feeling full of the Christmas spirit.

Family and isolation

Scrooge's isolation

At the beginning of the novella, Scrooge isolates himself and wants to be alone. The narrator tells us that he warns 'all human sympathy to keep its distance', suggesting that he doesn't want to connect emotionally to anyone. When his nephew, Fred, invites Scrooge to celebrate Christmas with his family he rejects him and says that there is no reason to be happy at this time of year. However, we soon begin to see the reasons why Scrooge may have isolated himself. The Ghost of Christmas Past creates sympathy for Scrooge when he shows him as 'a lonely boy' who is 'reading by a feeble fire'. Dickens' repetition of images of Scrooge's solitary* childhood shows us that he may be used to being alone and has accepted it, so this is why he isolates himself from society as a grown man.

Scrooge's decision to focus on money and himself means he has never had a family of his own. When Scrooge sees Belle with her family, he realises he will have no children to care for him in old age, and Dickens uses a metaphor* to show this using the seasons: 'a spring-time in the haggard winter of his life'. The child he could have had is compared to spring and Scrooge is compared to winter to show that his child would have made him feel young and refreshed like spring when he was nearing death, which is like winter when it is cold and there appears to be no life.

Similarly, the Ghost of Christmas Yet To Come shows Scrooge the consequences of living an isolated life where money is the priority rather than family when it shows him the body of the unknown man, which is left 'plundered and bereft, unwatched, unwept, uncared for'. There is no one to mourn the dead man because he has no family and this scene frightens Scrooge because he realises this may happen to him. The laundress* asks the other thieves why Scrooge wasn't more 'natural' when he was alive, showing how others believed that if Scrooge had been more sociable and caring then he would have had more people to care about him when he died.

Scrooge's attitude to family

At the beginning of the novella, Scrooge does not value family or relationships. He makes this clear when he scoffs at Fred for saying that he got married because he fell in love. The narrator says that Scrooge growled in return, as if that was 'the one thing in the world more ridiculous than a merry Christmas'. Scrooge believes a man should get married to improve his social or financial status and either marry for money or live alone and keep his money so he doesn't have to spend it on a family. Scrooge cannot understand why Bob Cratchit would celebrate Christmas when he has very little money and a large family who are expensive to feed. He mocks Bob's enthusiasm for Christmas when he mutters to himself with disbelief: '"My clerk, with fifteen shillings a week, and a wife and family, talking about a merry Christmas"'.

However, when the Ghost of Christmas Past reminds Scrooge of his nephew, Fred, we see for the first time that Scrooge may be beginning to understand how important family is. Scrooge is 'uneasy in his mind' thinking about Fred and the way he has treated him, suggesting that he is beginning to realise that family can bring happiness. This is prompted by the ghost showing him his close relationship with Fred's mother, Fan, when they were young, and Scrooge realises how much family meant to him when he was younger. It could be that he wants this feeling again.

At the end of the novella, Scrooge has realised the value of spending time with family. After he arrives at Fred's house on Christmas Day and asks Fred to let him in, the narrator comments on how happy the family celebration is: 'Wonderful party, wonderful games, wonderful unanimity, won-der-ful happiness!'. The repetition of the adjective* 'wonderful' emphasises how much everyone, including Scrooge, enjoys being together as a family to celebrate Christmas. Scrooge also has the chance to be the father figure he never was to his own children because to Tiny Tim 'he became a second father'. This shows that Scrooge knows he can still be supportive and caring like a father and both he and Tiny Tim will benefit. He has learnt from the ghosts how important family is and so now he values his own family and friends.

Family brings happiness

Fred understands the value of family and wants to include his uncle, Scrooge, in his family's Christmas celebrations when he says: '"Come! Dine with us tomorrow"'. His use of imperative verbs* to persuade Scrooge shows how strongly he feels about the family being together. The evidence of the joy that Fred and his family and friends experience because they are together is shown through their laughter as Fred 'laughed', Scrooge's niece 'laughed as heartily' and their friends 'roared out lustily'. Similarly, Belle is at the heart of a big family and, despite her life being loud and chaotic, she is happy and content, with a 'laughing face'. The Cratchit family are also happy because they are together at Christmas time and are 'happy, grateful, pleased with one another, and contented'. Family brings happiness for all of them, whether they are a large or small family or whether they have lots of money or are poor.

Dickens also describes how many other families are pleased to be with one another, creating a sense of community when he describes the children 'running out into the snow to meet their married sisters, brothers, cousins, uncles, aunts'. The miners, whom Scrooge visits with the Ghost of Christmas Present, include many generations and are 'a cheerful company assembled round a glowing fire'. Similarly, the sailors enjoy thinking about their family at Christmas time, even if they are not physically with them, as each one 'remembered those he cared for at a distance'. Dickens wants to show how family, wherever they are, can bring happiness, and ultimately this is the lesson that the ghosts want to teach Scrooge to prompt him to change.

Social responsibility*

Scrooge's social responsibility

Dickens presents the charity collectors as having a clear sense of social responsibility because they feel they should make "'some slight provision for the poor and destitute*'", especially at Christmas. Scrooge, by contrast, feels he has no social responsibility to help those living in poverty. He believes the government are responsible as he already pays them his taxes so that they can pay for the poor to live in prisons and workhouses*. He feels that he doesn't need to give to charity if the 1834 New Poor Law* is "'in full vigour'" and is already providing unemployed people with housing and food. Scrooge's comment that he "'can't afford to make idle people merry'" reflects many people's attitudes in Victorian times that those in poverty were lazy. Similarly, his view that poor people should die to "'decrease the surplus population'" echoes Thomas Malthus' opinion at the time. These are intended to shock the reader and make them think about their own attitude towards poverty.

Scrooge tells Belle that he focuses on money because he is afraid of being poor and says there is nothing "'so hard as poverty'". He believes that people like him who work hard to avoid poverty should not have to support those whom he believes are poor because they are lazy. However, this makes his lack of sympathy towards the poor even more shocking as he knows that they have the same fears as him but are less fortunate because they are stuck in their situation.

The Ghost of Christmas Yet To Come wants to teach Scrooge that the fate of Tiny Tim and those in poverty is the responsibility of those who have money. If affluent* people like Scrooge are willing to change, then poverty can be reversed. At the end of the novella, Scrooge accepts his social responsibility* towards the poor and begins to make amends when he gives to the charity collector '"a great many back-payments"'. Dickens uses the character Scrooge to convey how he hopes his readers will change their own attitude so that they focus less on themselves and think more about being charitable and helping those in poverty.

Extreme poverty and extreme affluence

Dickens gives many examples of people who are even poorer than the Cratchits and are living in extreme poverty, in order to show the reader the reality of having no money to buy food or clothes. He juxtaposes* the desperation of a group of homeless 'ragged men and boys' gathered round a fire to find warmth with the very affluent members of society celebrating Christmas when he describes how The Lord Mayor, in his 'mighty Mansion House, gave orders to his fifty cooks and butlers'. He uses this juxtaposition to highlight the difference between how the poor and the rich are spending the festive season. Similarly, Dickens devotes several long, descriptive paragraphs to the abundance* of food available at Christmas time, such as: 'the raisins were so plentiful and rare, the almonds so extremely white, the sticks of cinnamon so long and straight'. This again emphasises the divide between what the poor and the rich can afford to enjoy at Christmas.

Dickens uses a semantic field of wealth to convey the affluence of the businessmen at The Exchange* in the city who 'clinked the money in their pockets', 'looked at their watches' and played with their 'great gold seals'. This shows how rich some people in society are and how material possessions are important to them. In contrast to this, the Ghost of Christmas Yet To Come shows Scrooge a desperately poor part of town where the thieves go to sell Scrooge's possessions, where 'the ways were foul and narrow; the shops and houses wretched; the people half-naked, drunken, slipshod, ugly' and 'the whole quarter reeked with crime, with filth, and misery'. Dickens describes the extreme poverty in Victorian London to make the reader aware of the reality of the living conditions and prompt them to want to help.

Marley's attitude

Jacob Marley has learnt after his death that he should have helped others more, rather than focus on himself as he says: '"Mankind was my business. The common welfare was my business; charity, mercy, forbearance, and benevolence, were all my business"'. Marley repeats the word 'business' to emphasise that the welfare of people should have been more important to him than making money. Dickens uses a play on the word 'business' as it has two relevant definitions: it can mean work that makes a profit but it can also mean something a person takes an interest in. Therefore, Marley is saying that the 'business' he should have focused on was taking an interest in other people. He wishes he had noticed those who were less fortunate when he was alive, as he says he walked through crowds with his 'eyes turned down'. He did not look up to see the desperate need of the people around him.

Dickens criticises the government for not taking more social responsibility when he says that some of the phantoms*, like Marley, roaming the air regretting their actions in life 'might be guilty governments'. Dickens believed that the government could have done more to support the poor so by suggesting that they are ghosts he believes that in future they will realise that they did not take enough action.

Tiny Tim's death

Dickens includes the imagined death of Tiny Tim so that the Ghost of Christmas Yet To Come can shock Scrooge with what will happen if he does not change his selfish ways. Dickens wants to convey the consequences for those living in poverty and the emotional impact on their families if society does not do more to support the poor. He uses short sentences to create a serious atmosphere when Tiny Tim has died such as: 'Quiet. Very quiet', 'Surely they were very quiet!' and 'They were very quiet again'. These abrupt sentences, along with the repetition of the word 'quiet', contrast with the lively, jolly atmosphere at the Cratchits' house on Christmas Day and conveys how upset the family are. Mrs Cratchit tries to be brave for her other children and speaks 'in a steady, cheerful voice, that only faltered once'. Her attempts to be strong, even though she is devastated, make the scene even more emotional. Bob's grief is also clear, as he 'broke down all at once', showing how he is significantly affected by his son's death because they had such a close relationship. Although Tiny Tim's death is accepted by the Cratchits more easily than we would expect due to the high number of children who died young in Victorian times, his death is still a shock for the reader and, most importantly, Scrooge, who is prompted to change his ways.

Education / Ignorance and Want

Dickens intentionally juxtaposes* the joyful Christmas celebrations at Fred's house with the Ghost of Christmas Present revealing the two children, Ignorance and Want, to show the contrast between those with money and those in poverty. He describes the effect that poverty has had on the children before revealing that they are 'Ignorance' and 'Want', so that the reader wonders why they are suffering so badly and are 'wretched, abject, frightful, hideous, miserable'. The ghost says that the children belong to mankind because it is everyone's responsibility to help stop poverty. By naming the children, Dickens conveys how poverty is caused by lack of knowledge and the need of food, shelter and warmth. However, he suggests that Ignorance needs to be addressed by society first when the ghost says '"most of all beware this boy"', because providing knowledge and education means poor people then are able to help themselves out of poverty. The Ghost of Christmas Present warns that he sees '"Doom"' in the future if people do not take social responsibility for the poor, and ultimately society as a whole will suffer.

Change and redemption*

Scrooge's selfishness

The whole story centres on Scrooge's change from being a miserly*, avaricious*, selfish character to becoming generous, kind and socially responsible. This is also known as Scrooge's redemption. For Christians, this is when someone who has behaved badly needs forgiveness for their sins* in order to be saved. Scrooge is saved from experiencing Jacob Marley's fate, to roam the earth as a ghost regretting his actions, because he makes amends for his sins in time. Dickens introduces Scrooge as a 'covetous old sinner', so we know that he needs to be saved. These sins are made clear when he expresses his view that he doesn't feel he should help support the poor, whom he feels should die to "'decrease the surplus population'". It seems that Scrooge is so convinced of his opinion that he will never change.

Scrooge's potential to change

Dickens uses Marley to foreshadow* Scrooge's redemption: "'I am here tonight to warn you, that you have yet a chance and hope of escaping my fate'". If Marley can see how selfish he was when he was alive then it is possible that Scrooge will also see how his attitude should change. We first see evidence of Scrooge beginning to change when he is 'filled with gladness' when the Ghost of Christmas Past shows him his young friends greeting each other at Christmas. This hints that Scrooge will begin on his path to redemption with the help of the three ghosts. Dickens also foreshadows Scrooge's ability to change when Fan talks about their father and says he is "'so much kinder than he used to be'". If Scrooge's father can change then we believe that Scrooge has the ability to become a better person too. The young Scrooge's close relationship with Fan, his romantic relationship with Belle and his good relationship with his boss Mr Fezziwig all show how Scrooge was once capable of connecting with others and therefore could do again.

When Scrooge begs the Ghost of Christmas Present to tell him that Tiny Tim will live, his attitude towards those living in poverty has completely changed from when he said to solve poverty they should die. He begs for the ghost to tell him Tiny Tim "'will be spared'", showing how he cares about what happens to him. This suggests that now Scrooge has seen an example of those living in poverty, he will be more sympathetic and will want to help more people less fortunate than himself. Scrooge asks the Ghost of Christmas Yet To Come in desperation: "'Why show me this if I am past all hope?"' He realises that he has committed sins by being avaricious and selfish but he knows he has the potential to change and is desperate to be able to make amends.

Scrooge's lessons

Scrooge knows he has learnt important lessons from all of the three spirits which have made him want to become a better person, so he says: "'The Spirits of all Three shall strive within me. I will not shut out the lessons they teach'". At the beginning of the novella, Scrooge would not listen to anyone or let anyone in to his solitary world, whereas now he says he will not "'shut out'" what he has learnt from the ghosts. Scrooge has become more open to advice, and is happy to let people in.

Each of the ghosts show Scrooge people he has been connected to in order to demonstrate their lessons:

1. Mr Fezziwig teaches Scrooge be a generous employer
2. Fred and Fan teach him to value family
3. Belle teaches him that love is more important than money
4. The Cratchits teach him that poverty is about real people with real feelings
5. The thieves, the wealthy businessmen and the family who owe Scrooge money teach him that a selfish, greedy life leads to loneliness in death.

Scrooge learns the ultimate lesson at the climax* of the novella when the Ghost of Christmas Yet To Come shows him the 'neglected grave' bearing his name. Scrooge now understands that if he continues to lead an isolated life it will lead to unhappiness and loneliness in death, with no one to care for him. He realises that he needs to change if he wants to avoid the terrifying future that the ghost has shown him.

Scrooge's transformation

In the final stave, Scrooge aims to make amends for the sins he committed against others by being generous and friendly to those he is close to and to people in society in general. He chooses to change and fully redeems himself. When Scrooge says he is '"quite a baby"', Dickens suggests that he has the opportunity to begin his life again and live his life the way he should have done before he became so selfish. His kindness towards the Cratchits, his generosity to the poor and his attempt to reconnect with Fred all mirror the ways in which he was living selfishly at the beginning of the novella, so his transformation is complete. Scrooge is so full of the Christmas spirit that this has helped him to become a joyful person who behaves more positively and can contribute meaningfully to society. The narrator comments that 'it was always said of him, that he knew how to keep Christmas well', so we know that Scrooge has fully redeemed himself and has committed to the changes he has made and to being a better person.

Childhood

Scrooge as a child

Dickens presents childhood as a time of happiness and freedom when he describes Scrooge's friends from his younger days as being 'in great spirits'. Their jolly, cheerful attitude contrasts with Scrooge's loneliness and isolation as a boy when he was 'a solitary* child, neglected by his friends'. However, Scrooge escapes his isolation through the stories he reads. When the Ghost of Christmas Past shows him his younger self at school, Scrooge says excitedly: '"Why it's Ali Baba!... One Christmas time, when yonder solitary child was left here all alone, he did come"'. The characters in the stories gave the young Scrooge the company that he did not have with real people. This makes the reader feel sympathy for Scrooge because we realise that he did not have the happy, sociable childhood that children should have the opportunity to experience.

Dickens presents Belle's children's childhood as innocent, energetic and chaotic, and they are happy to be with each other and their parents. Dickens uses a series of exclamatory sentences to show their excitement when their father arrives home and has brought them Christmas presents and toys: 'The joy, the gratitude, and ecstasy!' This contrasts with Scrooge's childhood because he was neglected by his father when he left Scrooge at school, so the reader sees the consequences of relationships with parents on their children. Scrooge's neglect as a child gives us a reason for his selfish nature, so that we have some sympathy with him and want him to change and be redeemed.

The effects of poverty on childhood

The Victorians believed that childhood was a time of purity and innocence and children should have the freedom to play and not have to experience hardship. However, the reality for poor children was grim conditions for those who worked in factories and down the mines. Even children in the higher classes of society were treated like smaller versions of adults and made to dress and behave like them.

Dickens aims to shock a Victorian reader by personifying the effects of poverty through the innocent children Ignorance and Want, so that people can see the consequences of not being charitable or helping the poor to gain an education. The children are dehumanised* when the

Ghost says: "'It might be a claw, for the flesh there is upon it'" as the claw suggests they are like animals. This contrasts with the boys from Scrooge's childhood who are full of joy and happiness. Dickens wants to show how different children are born into different lives; some have money and some are poor, and this influences their childhood. He aims to show how it is not a child's choice to be poor and therefore it is the responsibility of those with money to support those who need help.

Although Ignorance and Want are not real children, they convey the idea that without education and financial support, people living in poverty cannot earn their own money and save enough to pull themselves out of poverty. This has serious consequences for society because if they are not given the opportunity to gain more skills, get a better job and earn more money, there will still be many people in poverty who need to be supported by society, either by the government or through charitable donations. 'Ignorance' is seen as the more important issue to address because if people are educated and earn more money then they can afford to buy food and clothes, which is 'Want'.

Dickens uses Tiny Tim to make his message even clearer – if the rich do not start to be more charitable, more young children living in poverty will die: "'If these shadows remain unaltered by the Future, the child will die'". Both Scrooge and the reader see the devastating consequences on both a child and their family if they do not have enough money to afford food, clothes, somewhere warm to live and, in Tiny Tim's case, access to health care which could prevent his death. Dickens hopes that by showing the reality of poverty for children, more people will be more charitable.

Progress and revision check

1. Which Ghost personifies 'the Christmas Spirit'?

2. Who holds a Christmas party for his employees?

3. Who says Scrooge should blame himself for his isolation when he dies?

4. List five people, or groups of people, who value family.

5. What does Belle say Scrooge is afraid of and why is this shocking?

6. List five people who Scrooge encounters to teach him a lesson.

7. Why does Dickens believe helping to prevent 'Ignorance' is more important than responding to 'Want' to help people in poverty?

8. How is Scrooge's attitude to Christmas different from Fred's?

9. How are Scrooge's childhood and Belle's children's childhood different?

10. How does Dickens use Tiny Tim's death to present his ideas about poverty?

~ Form, structure and language ~

Form

A Christmas Carol is a novella, which is shorter than a novel but longer than a short story. Dickens chose this form so he could relate his message that Christmas is a time of charity, kindness and family in a few words but with lots of detail.

The novella is a narrative* written in prose* – it tells a story and is written in everyday language without metrical structure* so that it is clear and easy to understand. This form usually has a main protagonist* who changes in some way and there is only time for setting the scene, the rising action and finally a conclusion.

It also takes the form of a ghost story. In Victorian times, these stories were traditionally told at Christmas. Dickens would have written A Christmas Carol so that it would be just the right length to be read aloud in a short time.

Dickens' choice of the title A Christmas Carol suggests that the novella shares the characteristics of a carol:

- It is to be read aloud at Christmas time
- It has a religious message
- It should make the readers feel festive but they should learn from it

The novella is divided into five staves. A stave is another word for a stanza or verse, so this also suggests that the story is like a carol which is composed of verses. A stave is also a word for the five parallel lines which musical notes are written on, so by organising the novella into five staves, Dickens emphasises its light-hearted nature and that, like carols, it is to be read aloud to families and friends at Christmas.

Structure

Exposition, Rising action, Climax*, Resolution

The novella's five staves help the reader to understand the plot. Each stave adds more tension to the story and builds on the one that came before. Dickens chose this structure to engage the reader and make them want to find out whether Scrooge does change and become more charitable and less isolated.

Stave	Structure	What happens
One	Exposition	Introduces us to the setting of the story and Scrooge, the main protagonist. We also learn the central conflict, which is Scrooge's attitude to Christmas and his relationships with the other characters.
Two	Rising action	Shows us Scrooge's past. The Ghost of Christmas Past warns Scrooge that he must listen to him.
Three	Rising action	Shows us the present. The Ghost of Christmas Present warns Scrooge that he must listen to him.

Four	Climax	The Ghost of Christmas Yet To Come shows Scrooge his potential future, and the climax is when the name on the gravestone is revealed to be Scrooge's. The stave ends with a cliffhanger*, as both the reader and Scrooge are unsure whether he will have the chance to redeem himself.
Five	Resolution	Gives us the resolution of the story where Scrooge is transformed and promises to celebrate Christmas and live a more charitable and generous life.

The three ghosts

Dickens uses the three ghosts as a way to structure the novella and chart Scrooge's progression from a miserly*, selfish old man to a kind and generous person. We are shown why Scrooge has become so focused on money (the Ghost of Christmas Past), the ways he could be like other people at Christmas (the Ghost of Christmas Present) and what will happen if he does not change (the Ghost of Christmas Yet To Come). Dickens chose to do this so the reader can see how Scrooge gradually changes as he learns lessons from each of the three ghosts.

Symmetrical structure*

The novella has a symmetrical structure, as many of the events of the first stave are revisited in the final stave but now show how Scrooge has changed. Dickens chooses this structure to demonstrate that Scrooge's transformation is complete.

Stave One	Stave Five
Scrooge is rude to everyone and won't have anything to do with Christmas	Scrooge is friendly to everyone and wishes them all a "Merry Christmas"
Scrooge treats Bob Cratchit poorly by making him work in freezing conditions	Scrooge ensures the office is kept warm by buying more coal for the fire
Scrooge is annoyed that he has to pay Bob Cratchit for his day off on Christmas Day	Scrooge gives Bob Cratchit a pay rise
Scrooge rejects the charity collectors' requests for donations	Scrooge gives generously to the charity collector to make up for years of not giving any money
Scrooge rejects Fred's request to join him and his family to celebrate Christmas	Scrooge decides to accept Fred's invitation and takes part in the family celebrations

Time

The story is non-chronological* and includes flashbacks. Although the main part of the story is set in the present, we are then transported to Scrooge's past, to other places around the world in the present and then to the imaginary future. Within each of these times the ghosts move around swiftly to different times. The Ghost of Christmas Past even moves forwards to Belle and her family in the future which is actually happening in Scrooge's present. This use of time allows Dickens to give us a detailed impression of Scrooge and why he needs to change his ways.

The bell which tolls at the beginning of Stave Two signals the first ghost's visit and the time: 1am. However, Scrooge fell asleep after 2am, and each of the ghosts actually visits him in the same night. Dickens plays with the time so that Scrooge is able to wake on Christmas Day and has the chance to make the changes he needs to. Even though this is not logically believable, the reader is able to go along with it because they know it is a supernatural story and everything is not as it seems.

Language

Narrative voice*

The narrative voice is the person who is telling the story and we see the events unfold from their viewpoint. Although Dickens directly addresses the reader in the preface to the story, the narrator of the actual events is not Dickens.

The type of narrator Dickens chooses is an intrusive narrator*. This allows Dickens to comment on the characters and their actions and to make moral and political points without taking responsibility as the narrator, even though he is the author of the book. This makes it seem like it is someone else who is criticising the government and wealthy people for the way they treat the poor. The readers are more likely to respond positively to suggestions that they should be more charitable and generous than if it was a story where Dickens was telling them to change.

Dickens also gives the intrusive narrator a conversational, cheerful tone so that the reader engages with him from the beginning. The narrator directly addresses the reader when he says: 'You will therefore permit me to repeat, emphatically, that Marley was dead as a doornail'. By then going on to discuss whether his use of a simile to compare Marley to a doornail is appropriate, the intrusive narrator is building a trusting relationship with the reader so that when he introduces Scrooge as a 'covetous old sinner' we believe him and dislike Scrooge.

As the novella progresses, the intrusive narrator continues to express his views and opinions. For example, he comments on how he would have liked to be part of Belle's happy, chaotic family: 'What would I not have given to be one of them!'. By directly addressing the reader the intrusive narrator keeps the reader on his side and therefore guides them through Scrooge's transformation so that in the end we are pleased that Scrooge has changed and that the novella has a happy ending.

Metaphors*

Dickens uses metaphors in the novella to create a sinister, gloomy atmosphere through his description of the weather in the area of the city where Scrooge works on Christmas Eve. When he describes the fog as 'pouring in at every chink and keyhole', this represents how people who share Scrooge's negative, miserly* attitude are everywhere, in many of the city's houses. The verb 'pour' gives the impression of something that is unstoppable so Dickens is saying how difficult it is to change people's selfish ways, but this makes Scrooge's transformation more satisfying.

Dickens also uses a metaphor which adds to the sinister mood when he says that 'the houses opposite were mere phantoms'. He compares the buildings to ghostly figures, implying that they are difficult to see because the fog is so thick. This suggests that nothing can be seen clearly and therefore there is a sense of mystery and potentially a threat. Dickens also uses the word 'phantoms' to foreshadow* Marley's visit to Scrooge and to hint at the supernatural element of the story. Phantoms are seen as unpredictable, which creates a tense mood. Dickens almost wants the reader to be on guard, like Scrooge is when he is visited by the spirits, and so they may also be more open to Dickens' message.

Pathetic fallacy*

Dickens uses pathetic fallacy to represent Scrooge's transformation. He is presented as a cold and unfeeling person at the beginning of the story, when the weather is described as 'cold, bleak, biting weather: foggy withal'. This represents how Scrooge shows no emotion towards other people, including his family and those in society who live in poverty. Fog connotes a sense of blindness, which could show how Scrooge doesn't want to see the reality of poverty. When Dickens says 'the fog and darkness thickened', we get a sense that this selfish attitude in society is getting worse rather than improving over time.

However, this contrasts with the weather at the end of the story when Scrooge changes: 'No fog, no mist; clear, bright, jovial, stirring'. Dickens uses the disappearance of the fog to represent how Scrooge can now clearly see what his responsibility is towards the poor. This change in the weather also reflects Dickens' message that everyone benefits when the wealthy in society begin to be more charitable, as positivity creates more positivity.

Personification*

Dickens uses personification throughout the novella to emphasise a positive, cheerful atmosphere. He creates a festive Christmas feeling when the Ghost of Christmas Present takes Scrooge onto the streets of the city on Christmas morning. Dickens describes the onions as 'winking from their shelves in wanton slyness' and the oranges and lemons as begging 'to be carried home in paper bags'. This gives the impression that the food is also alive with the Christmas spirit and wants to be involved in the celebrations. Dickens aims to convey to richness and abundance of food that those with money have, in order to set up a contrast with his depressing, shocking descriptions of those in poverty later in the story.

Similarly, Dickens uses personification to create an energetic and excited atmosphere when he says that the potatoes at the Cratchits house 'knocked loudly at the saucepan-lid to be let out and peeled'. The family are all enjoying preparing for Christmas dinner together and their excitement is mirrored by the potatoes which seem to be as keen to be released from the pan as the children are to eat them. Dickens creates a lively tone to convey how happy the Cratchits are, despite having very little money to afford an extravagant Christmas dinner.

However, Dickens also uses personification to make a negative, gloomy mood more intense. He describes the churchyard where Scrooge's potential future grave is as 'choked up with too much burying; fat with repleted appetite'. This suggests that the churchyard is packed so tightly with dead bodies that it is unable to breathe and nothing can grow, flourish or survive there: it is the epitome* of death. The fact that it is full and fat implies that it has consumed the dead bodies and cannot eat any more, again conveying the idea that there is no room for any more graves. Dickens wants to create a gloomy, depressing setting to emphasise how serious his message is about the consequences for society when people don't think about poverty.

Similarly, when he describes the 'gruff old bell' in the church tower as 'always peeping slily down at Scrooge', the reader gets a sense that Scrooge is being watched by the bell which disapproves of his selfish actions. Furthermore, the fact that the bell belongs to the church emphasises the idea that Scrooge is not behaving like a Christian should. Dickens uses the bell to represent how God does not tolerate Scrooge's actions and to show how God is watching everyone and judging the choices they make, which may prompt the reader to change their selfish ways too.

Similes*

Dickens uses similes to demonstrate Scrooge's transformation. He introduces Scrooge as a lonely man who has isolated himself from society, when he describes him as 'solitary as an oyster'. Dickens compares Scrooge to an oyster because they live alone in their shell and are difficult to open. In the same way, people such as Fred find it hard to get close to Scrooge as he won't let anyone form a relationship with him. This could possibly be because he lost his sister, the only person with whom he had a close connection. In addition, oysters sometimes contain a pearl so Dickens could be suggesting that inside this hard exterior there is the good, loving person Scrooge once was – he just needs to come out of his shell.

At the end of the novella, Dickens uses similes again to show how Scrooge has changed. Scrooge uses four similes to describe how he feels when he wakes up and realises it is Christmas morning: 'as light as a feather... as happy as an angel... as merry as a school-boy... as giddy as a drunken man'. This conveys his cheerful, jolly mood as he compares himself to objects or people that represent purity, youth and delight. The reader can imagine Scrooge dancing around the room in the same way that they can picture a youthful school-boy playing, or a mildly drunken man behaving merrily. This description of youth and positivity links to the idea of Scrooge's rebirth – he has been given another chance to live a life which can benefit those who are less fortunate than him and has therefore been born again.

Adjectives*

Dickens often bombards his reader with a list of adjectives in order make his descriptions have more impact. The children Ignorance and Want are described as 'wretched, abject, frightful, hideous, miserable' and 'yellow, meagre, ragged, scowling, wolfish'. Dickens wants the reader to understand the full extent of the impact of poverty on the children. The adjectives 'wretched and miserable' show how significantly they have been affected emotionally, while 'frightful and hideous' convey how they are almost unbearable to look at. Dickens dehumanises* the children through the adjectives 'wolfish' and 'scowling' suggesting that they have become like animals due to lack of food and any form of education.

He also uses a list of adjectives to describe the poor people in the most deprived area of London as 'half-naked, drunken, slipshod, ugly'. These shocking, harsh words suggest that they are unable to afford clothes to keep them warm so that they appear indecent, and that they are addicted to alcohol which is seen as a sin in the eyes of Christians. 'Slipshod' connotes a careless attitude showing how they cannot see any opportunities in their future so they have almost given up on life, and the adjective 'ugly' suggests that poverty has made them repulsive to look at. These descriptions of Ignorance and Want and the people in poverty are intended to appal the reader and make them want help the poor in society.

In the same way, Dickens describes the body of the unknown dead man as 'plundered and bereft, unwatched, unwept, uncared for', to emphasise how much the man has lost as a consequence of living an isolated and selfish life. 'Plundered and bereft' suggests there is nothing left, which could represent that once a person's material possessions have gone all that is left is the memory of their good deeds and positive relationships from when they were alive. However, in the case of the unknown man, there is nothing left because all he cared about when he was alive was money and wealth. Dickens also repeats the prefix 'un' to emphasise how there is no one to mourn the man after a life which was full of avarice* and greed.

Repetition

Dickens uses repetition to emphasise the change in Scrooge's character from the beginning to the end of the story. He emphasises how Marley and Scrooge isolated themselves from society when he says how Scrooge was the only person who dealt with Marley's death: 'Scrooge was his sole executor, his sole administrator, his sole assign, his sole residuary legatee, his sole friend and sole mourner'. By repeating the adjective 'sole', which has connotations of loneliness and selfishness, Dickens conveys how no one else but Scrooge cared about Marley's death, suggesting that when Marley was alive he was only concerned with himself. As we know that Scrooge and Marley were partners and were both focused on business and profit, Dickens foreshadows what the Ghost of Christmas Yet To Come warns Scrooge: if he lives the same way as Marley he will suffer the same consequences.

Dickens also uses repetition when he introduces Scrooge's cold-hearted character: 'No warmth could warm him… no wind that blew was bitterer than he, no falling snow was more intent upon its purpose… no pelting rain less open to entreaty'. The repetition of the word 'no' shows how absolutely nothing is as bitter, cold and unwelcoming as Scrooge, even the most extreme weather conditions. This contrasts to the end of the story when the narrator says that Scrooge 'became as good a friend, as good a master, and as good a man, as the good old city knew, or any other good old city, town or borough, in the good old world'. The repetition of the adjective 'good' shows how Scrooge has fully redeemed himself as he is not just a friend or boss but someone who is respected and admired because he behaves correctly and responsibly. The adjective 'good' is then extended to describe locations, implying that if someone chooses to act responsibly then there is a positive knock-on effect on everything around them.

Progress and revision check

1. What is the form of A Christmas Carol?

2. What is a stave?

3. What happens at the climax of the novel?

4. What is the name of the structure describing the way Stave Five mirrors Stave One?

5. What type of narrator does Dickens use and why?

6. What atmosphere does Dickens create through his use of metaphors?

7. What does the use of pathetic fallacy represent?

8. What is the effect of Dickens' personification of food?

9. What do the similes show about Scrooge at the end of the story?

10. Why does Dickens use lists of adjectives in his descriptions?

~ Key quotations and glossary ~

Key quotations

Characters

Scrooge

'hard and sharp as flint'

'solitary as an oyster'

"If they would rather die…they had better do it, and decrease the surplus population."

'I am as light as a feather, I am as happy as an angel, I am as merry as a school-boy. I am as giddy as a drunken man."

'He became as good a friend, as good a master, and as good a man, as the good old city knew.'

The Ghost of Christmas Past

'From the crown of its head there sprung a bright clear jet of light.'

'what was light one instant, at another time was dark'

The Ghost of Christmas Present

'sparkling eye… cheery voice…joyful air!'

'bore a glowing torch, in shape not unlike Plenty's horn'

The Ghost of Christmas Yet To Come

'a solemn phantom, draped and hooded, coming, like a mist along the ground, towards him'

'seemed to scatter gloom and mystery'

Jacob Marley

'it was made of cash-boxes, keys, padlocks, ledgers, deeds and heavy purses'

"I am here tonight to warn you, that you have yet a chance and hope of escaping my fate."

Fred

'all in a glow; his face was ruddy and handsome; his eyes sparkled'

Christmas is "a good time: a kind, forgiving, charitable, pleasant time."

The Cratchits

'Eked out by the apple-sauce and mashed potatoes, it was a sufficient dinner for the whole family.'

'Happy, grateful, pleased with one another, and contented with the time.'

Tiny Tim

'bore a little crutch and had his limbs supported by an iron frame'

'hoped the people saw him in the church, because he was a cripple, and it might be pleasant to them to remember upon Christmas Day, who made lame beggars walk and blind men see'

Themes

The Christmas spirit

'to think of people below them as if they really were fellow passengers to the grave'

'fuel was heaped upon the fire; and the warehouse was as snug, and warm, and dry, and bright as a ball-room'

Family and Isolation

'a lonely boy… reading by a feeble fire'

'Wonderful party, wonderful games, wonderful unanimity, won-der-ful happiness!'

Social responsibility

"Mankind was my business. The common welfare was my business; charity, mercy, forbearance, and benevolence, were all my business."

'the ways were foul and narrow; the shops and houses wretched; the people half-naked, drunken, slipshod, ugly'

Change and Redemption

"The Spirits of all Three shall strive within me. I will not shut out the lessons they teach."

'it was always said of him, that he knew how to keep Christmas well'

Childhood

"It might be a claw, for the flesh there is upon it"

"If these shadows remain unaltered by the Future, the child will die."

Glossary

Abundance: a very large amount of something

Adjective: a word that describes a noun

Affluent: wealthy or rich

Allegory: a story that includes characters, places and events which are used as symbols to represent ideas linked to morals, religion or politics that teach the reader a lesson

Avarice/ Avaricious: extreme greed for money

Charwoman: a cleaner

Cholera: an infectious disease with no known cure in Victorian times

Cliffhanger: when the ending of part of a story is sudden and the character is left in a difficult situation without knowing what will happen next

Climax: the part of a story where the tension reaches its highest point

Dehumanise: to make someone seem less like a human

Destitute: extremely poor

Dialogue: a conversation between two or more people

Dramatic irony: when the reader knows something a character doesn't know

Emit: give out

Empathy: the ability to understand what another person is experiencing

Enlightened: provided with information, understanding and the true facts

Epitome: perfect example

The Exchange/ 'Change: The Royal Exchange in London where trading took place

Foil: a character who contrasts with another character

Foreshadowing: a hint about something that will happen later in the story

Idol: something that is admired and worshipped like a god

Ignorance: lack of knowledge and understanding

Imperative verbs: verbs which give a command or instruction

The Industrial Revolution: the time period when the process of change in industry from agriculture to factories occurred

Inferiority: having a lower status or social position

Intrusive narrator: a narrator who comments on characters and their actions

Juxtaposition/ to juxtapose: placing two contrasting ideas next to each other for effect

Laundress: a woman who washes clothes for a living

Lame: a disability where someone cannot walk

Metaphor/ metaphorically: Compares one thing to something else that has a similar characteristic, stating that something 'is' something else

Metrical structure: a specific rhythm with a pattern of beats

Milliner: someone who makes hats

Miser/ miserly: a person who spends as little money as possible

Narrative: a spoken or written description of events, or a story

Narrative voice: the person who is telling the story

New Poor Law: the law that aimed to support those in poverty by giving them food and shelter in return for work

Non-chronological: not occurring in the logical order of time

Old Scratch: a nickname for the devil

Oxymoron: when two words placed next to each other, which appear have opposite meanings, create an effect

Pathetic fallacy: when human feelings and actions are given to objects. It can also be used to represent a character's mood, feelings and personality

Personification: when an object is given human characteristics

Phantom: a ghost

Portly: respected and admirable

Prose: writing in everyday language without metrical structure

Protagonist: the main character in a novel

Redemption: being saved from sin or from behaving in the wrong way

Sabbatarianism: the belief that Sunday is a holy day when no one should work

Secular: not connected to religion

Simile: compares one thing to something else that has a similar characteristic, using the word 'like' or 'as'

Sin: behaving incorrectly against God's teachings

Social responsibility: choosing to support those less fortunate in society

Solitary: existing alone

Spiritualism: the belief in the ability to communicate with the dead

Superlative: something that has more of a certain quality than anything else, for example, biggest, best or most

Supernatural: something that cannot be scientifically explained such as ghosts, magic and miracles

Symbol/ symbolism: a physical object that represents an idea, thought or experience

Symmetrical structure: where events mirror each other

Treadmill: a punishment in prisons where machines were powered by people walking

Undertaker's man: an assistant to the person who organises a funeral

Want: need for food, clothes and shelter

Workhouse: where those who could not earn their own money to support themselves worked in return for food and shelter

~ Revision and exam help ~

Exam preparation

Your best preparation for the exam is to get to know the novella as well as you can. This does not mean just the plot, but all the analysis, characters, themes, form, structure and language that are covered in this guide. However, in order to do this to the best of your ability, you need to know what the exam is testing you on.

Assessment objectives

Assessment objectives simply means "what you are being tested on". The exam will assess you on four main skills:

Assessment Objective	What It says	What It means
AO1	Read, understand and respond to texts. Students should be able to: • maintain a critical style and develop an informed personal response • use textual references, including quotations, to support and illustrate interpretations	• This checks if you have understood the main elements of the **plot, characters, themes and relationships** in the text. • You need to create **arguments based on your personal opinions** of the characters, themes and relationships. • You need to use **quotations and examples** that prove the arguments you are making.

AO2	Analyse the language, form and structure used by a writer to create meanings and effects, using relevant subject terminology where appropriate	<ul><li>You need to back up the arguments you are making by analysing **how language, form and structure help to prove your point**.</li><li>You need to analyse **the writer's purpose or intention in using these techniques** and what they are trying to make the reader think, learn or feel.</li><li>You need to use **the correct terms** when identifying language, form and structure.</li></ul>
AO3	Show understanding of the relationships between texts and the contexts in which they were written	<ul><li>You need to explain **how the writer was influenced** by the following during the time that the text was written:<ul><li>What was happening **in society and politics**</li><li>What was happening **in literature**</li><li>What was happening **to the author personally.**</li></ul></li></ul>

AO4	Use a range of vocabulary and sentence structures for clarity, purpose and effect, with accurate spelling and punctuation	• This checks that you are using: wide-ranging and ambitious vocabulary; simple, compound and complex sentences correctly; that your spelling and punctuation are accurate. • 5% of the marks in English Literature are for spelling, grammar and punctuation, so make sure you proof-read your work to get these marks.

Mapping your revision – The "Journey"

Every character, theme and relationship goes on a journey through the text; this is not a physical journey, but what this means is that they will either change, grow or develop from the beginning to the end of the text. For a clear way to revise, follow these steps:

1. Choose a character, theme or relationship to revise. The sub-headings in this guide are a great place to start. Now find the important pages for your chosen area of revision in this guide. As an example, the character Scrooge is completed below.

2. Write down what you think the writer's overall purpose is for this character/ theme/relationship using the information you read in the guide. For example:

   "Dickens' purpose for Scrooge was to use him as an example of the upper class people living in London, who represented greed and selfishness, rather than the Christmas spirit."

3. The first question that you should ask yourself is: "How does the character/ theme/relationship change, grow or develop during the text?" Now, plot these on an arrow that represents the beginning to the end. Choose what you think are the top five key moments:

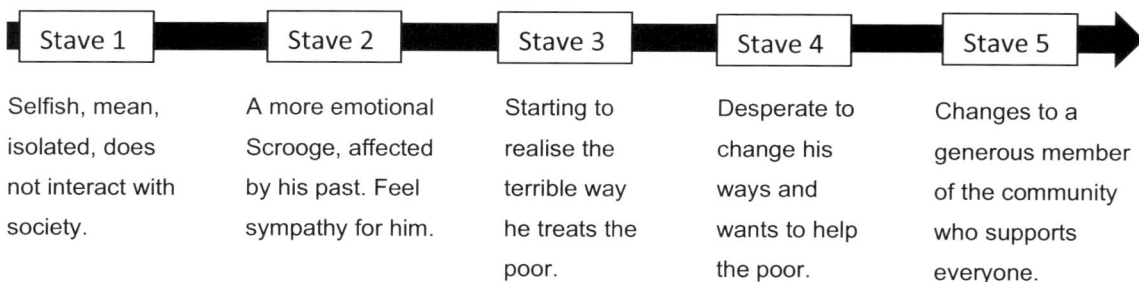

Stave 1	Stave 2	Stave 3	Stave 4	Stave 5
Selfish, mean, isolated, does not interact with society.	A more emotional Scrooge, affected by his past. Feel sympathy for him.	Starting to realise the terrible way he treats the poor.	Desperate to change his ways and wants to help the poor.	Changes to a generous member of the community who supports everyone.

4. Choose key quotations that are the **best** example of what you have said about the character/theme/relationship. For example:

> Stave 1

Selfish, mean, isolated, does not interact with society.

⬇

"solitary as an oyster"

5. Analyse the language, form or structure of your chosen quotation. You could also choose to discuss the importance of where this scene appears in the text. For example:

"solitary as an oyster"

⬇

Simile: compares Scrooge to an oyster because they live alone in their shell and are difficult to prise open.

6. Add important contextual information that you think has influenced the writer in making the choices that they have made. You may not need this for every key moment you have chosen. There is also no need to repeat yourself! For example:

> Stave 1

Selfish, mean, isolated, does not
interact with society.

⬇

A reflection of upper-class people like Malthus who
believed that the only way to decrease overpopulation
was to let poor people die.

Once you have done this, you have revised everything that you need to know about the character/theme/relationship, and you have used this revision guide in a really meaningful way. It also means that you should have the information you need to answer an exam question on your chosen area of revision.

Remember: if you know the text well enough, there is nothing you can't answer!

The exam question

The type of question that you will be asked will depend on which exam board your school is entering you for. The most popular exam boards that examine A Christmas Carol are:

Exam Board	What Paper it will be on	What you will be asked to do in the exam
AQA	Paper 1	There is no choice. Answer one question about a particular character/theme/relationship in the extract and the text as a whole.
Edexcel	Paper 2	There is no choice. There are two parts to the question: A and B. Answer Part A on the language, form and structure used to describe a topic in the extract and Part B on a particular character/ theme/relationship in the text as a whole.
Eduquas	Component 2	There is no choice. Answer one question about a particular character/theme/relationship in the extract and the text as a whole.

Remember: it is important to know which exam board you are studying! Double check with your teacher so that you revise correctly.

Answering the question

1. Read the question twice so that you fully understand what it is asking you to do.

2. Underline the character/theme/relationship that you are being asked to answer on. This will be the focus of your answer. Underline any other key words and phrases that are important.

   Hint: every year the wording of the question will stay the same. The only thing that will change will be the focus of the question; the changing words are what you should be underlining as this will tell you exactly what you need to answer on.

3. If you are asked to answer on an extract, read it through twice. The first time, just read it through so you understand what is happening. The second time, underline important words or phrases that will help you to answer the question.

> How does Dickens present Scrooge's attitude towards the poor in the novella?
>
> Refer to the following extract in your answer.

Your focus is on Scrooge, specifically about how he responds to the poor.

Important exam question language

Exam questions are worded in a similar way every year. This is why it is important that you know exactly what they mean.

Key Word	What it means
Explore / Explain	This means that you should make three or four points about the character, theme or relationship so that you give enough detail.
Attitudes to	You are being asked to discuss the way a character/lots of characters think and feel about a particular theme, which may show in the way they behave towards something.
How Dickens uses	"How" asks you to look at Dickens' techniques, such as the language, form and structure of the text, to support the arguments you have made.
How far you agree	You will be given a statement and you can choose to agree or disagree (or both!) with this statement, using evidence from the text.
Refer to	This means what you should mention specifically in your answer.

Planning Your Answer

This is one of the most important parts of what you will do in the exam! The majority of the marks you get are based on whether you develop your argument and you cannot do that if you haven't planned. It will also help you feel calm and less overwhelmed in the exam. Planning also helps you to choose the best ideas that match your argument, rather than the first one that comes into your head.

The step-by-step approach to the five-minute plan

1. Brainstorm or bullet point everything you remember about the character, theme or relationship you have been asked about. Empty your head! This should take no longer than thirty seconds. Make sure you include at least one idea from the extract if you have been given one.

2. Write down the numbers 1-5 on your planning sheet, leaving space to jot your ideas down. This will be the basic structure of your answer. This is what you should write beside each number:

    1: Write a summary of the journey that the character, theme or relationship takes during the text. Just write one or two sentences.
    2-4: Use your brainstorming from Step 1 to choose the three key moments in the text that demonstrate the argument you created. You will have loads in your brainstorm, but you must now choose **the best ideas**. Remember, if there is an extract, make sure to include at least one idea from the extract.
    5: Sum up your main point and write down what you think the author's purpose was for creating the character, theme or relationship like this.

3. Go back over your plan and include the best quotations for **2-4**. You do not need any additional quotations in your introduction or conclusion.

4. Read over your plan. Add any context or language techniques that you remember from your revision. This way, when you use your

plan to write your answer, you won't forget to add this important information. You might also want to juggle around the paragraphs if you think they would work better in another order.

Key moment from Stave 1 (Step 2)

Example plan for how Scrooge is presented in A Christmas Carol

1. Scrooge – a spiritual journey. Goes from being selfish, mean and greedy to caring about others in society.

2. Beginning: cold-hearted: rejects the charity workers – "Are there no prisons? Are there no workhouses?" – links to the Malthusian theory of surplus population and the Poor Law. Rhetorical questions = dismissing them.

3. Changes especially when he deals with Present: repeats his words to him "Are there no prisons? Are there no workhouses?" Point of realisation for Scrooge that the Poor Law is not effective.

4. His redemption at the end: symmetrical structure emphasises this – becomes a "second father" to Tiny Tim. Juxtaposes Stave 1 when he didn't help the needy.

5. Dickens' purpose for Scrooge is to use him as a metaphor for the upper class people living in London, who represented greed and selfishness, rather than community spirit and how he wants them to change for the better and embrace community.

Best quotation to show his change (Step 3)

Language analysis is included using the correct term (Step 4)

Golden rules of planning

1. Only give yourself five minutes at the beginning of each question. The plan itself doesn't get any marks so any longer will just eat into your essay-writing time.

2. Look back at your plan before you write a paragraph. This will keep you on track and will make sure you don't forget anything you want to say.

3. Use a full page to plan out your response. You don't have to worry about running out of space in your exam booklet; you can always ask for more paper.

Writing introductions

Your introduction is the first impression you will make on an examiner, so it is important that it has an impact to get you the grade you deserve.

Your introduction is Step 1 from your plan, which you will now develop:

> **1:** Write a summary of the journey that the character, theme or relationship takes during the text.

- Make sure that you answer the question in detail, talking about how the character, theme or relationship changes, grows or develops from the beginning to the end.

- Make sure that you list the points that you plan to argue – your examiner will then have a really clear idea what you are going to talk about.

- Explain the author's purpose for this character, theme or relationship. What message are they trying to get across to their readers by including this?

- You could start by using the words from the question in your introduction to help you begin.

Example Introduction: Explore how the character of Scrooge is presented in A Christmas Carol

Dickens presents Scrooge as a character who goes on a spiritual journey from the beginning to the end of the novella. The whole novella focuses on his redemption, from being ignorant of society's problems because he is too selfish to care in Stave One, to slowly realising the error of his ways in Stave Three, to becoming enlightened and willing to play his part in looking after society's most vulnerable in Stave Five. Perhaps Dickens is trying to teach the upper-class people in society, whom Scrooge represents, about the importance of looking after others, especially at Christmas time.

Writing main paragraphs

This is the section where you are going to get the bulk of your marks. This is the opportunity for you to expand on what you have said in your introduction and develop your arguments in detail.

Your main paragraphs are Steps 2-4 of your plan, which you will now develop:

> **2-4:** Use your brainstorming from Step 1 to choose the three key moments in the text that demonstrate the argument you created. You will have loads in your brainstorm, but you must now choose **the best ideas**. Remember, if there is an extract, make sure to include at least one idea from the extract.

Paragraph structure

AO1: Answer the question. How/why does the character / theme change from previously?

AO3: Links made to context

AO1: Short, embedded quotation and explanation of how the quotation proves the point

AO2: Analysis of language or structure to support argument

AO2: Writer's purpose – why has Dickens included this scene / character and what is the effect?

The paragraph structure to the left will help you to develop your argument fully to make sure that you meet all of the assessment objectives.

AO1: Your argument and opinions and your ability to back up your arguments with evidence from the text.

AO2: Your analysis of language and structure, as well as your explanation of why the writer makes the decisions they do.

AO3: Your explanation of how the text links to the context. This is done best when it is linked to your argument.

Example main paragraph: Explore how the character of Scrooge is presented in A Christmas Carol (argument from Stave Five)

AO1: argument	In Stave Five, Dickens presents Scrooge as a new man and a complete contrast to the old Scrooge; he is more grateful and caring. He no longer represents the
AO3: context linked	stereotypical Victorian upper class man whose thoughts are dominated by money and financial gain. He now represents what Dickens wanted to achieve, which is a more socially responsible society. Dickens describes how
AO1: quotation	Scrooge is excited to be part of Fred's party as the narrator describes the "Wonderful party, wonderful games, wonderful unanimity, won-der-ful happiness" that Scrooge sees all around him. Dickens repeats the adjective "wonderful"; this shows his life is better now and
AO2: language analysis	Scrooge is full of excitement and happiness because he was busy isolating himself before. The dashes in the final "won-der-ful" emphasise each individual syllable, almost revelling in the word as its repetition shows the
AO2: writer's purpose	remarkable change in Scrooge's behaviour. The reader is left with the impression that if Scrooge can change so quickly then anyone can change for the better. Dickens demonstrates that he wants society to be equal and fair, and Scrooge's change reflects this.

Dos and don'ts when writing main paragraphs

Do

- Link your paragraphs together to create a "flow" in your essay. Refer back to what you said previously.

- Write more than one sentence for each part of the paragraph structure. Explain yourself fully!

- Give more than one interpretation of language/structure if you can and only if it links to the argument you are making.

- Make sure that every part of the structure refers back to the first sentence and your overall argument.

Don't

- Repeat context that you have said before. It is not necessary to put context in every paragraph if it means you are just repeating yourself.

- Use the same sentence starters for all three paragraphs. Your writing will sound like you are filling in the blanks!

- Forget to always ask yourself "why". Why has the character changed? Why has the writer used that language technique? Why does that quotation prove your point?

Writing conclusions

If your introduction is your first impression, then the conclusion is the last impression you give the examiner before they award you a mark. That's why it needs to be punchy, impactful and meaningful!

Your conclusion is Step 5 from your plan, which you will now develop:

> **5:** Sum up your main point and write down what you think the author's purpose is for creating the character, theme or relationship like this.

- Make sure that you summarise the journey that the character or theme has been on in one to two sentences.
- Explain the author's overall purpose for this character, theme or relationship. What is the key message they are trying to get across?
- Don't introduce any new ideas – this is your opportunity to summarise your key arguments.

Example Conclusion: Explore how the character of Scrooge is presented in A Christmas Carol

In conclusion, Dickens reveals a fully changed character to his readers by the end of Stave Five. Scrooge has undergone such a dramatic change that he is now the complete opposite of the Scrooge we meet in Stave One. Dickens' purpose for Scrooge is to use him as a metaphor for the upper class people living in London, who represent greed and selfishness, rather than community spirit, and how Dickens wanted them to change for the better and embrace community, just like Scrooge was able to do.

Using quotations in the exam

The whole point of having quotations in your response is to prove the arguments that you make. However, that doesn't mean you have to learn the whole novella off by heart!

Tips and tricks for using quotations

1. Look at the key quotations on page 58 of this revision guide.
2. Choose the quotations that **best** prove the point you are trying to make about the character, theme or relationship.
3. Keep your quotations to a couple of words or a phrase. Don't write long amounts of text in your answer. Just stick to the part that actually proves what you are saying.
4. Try to embed your quotations into the sentence. This simply means making the quotations part of your own sentence.
5. Always use quotation marks!

Not embedded:

Dickens describes how Scrooge is excited to be part of Fred's party. This can be seen in the quotation: "Wonderful party, wonderful games, wonderful unanimity, won-der-ful happiness".

Embedded:

Dickens describes how Scrooge is excited to be part of Fred's party as he describes the "Wonderful party, wonderful games, wonderful unanimity, won-der-ful happiness" that he saw all around him.

Here is another example:

Not embedded:

In Stave One Dickens presents Scrooge as a man who does not care about the poor and feels like he doesn't have any responsibility towards them. This can be seen in the quotation: "If they would rather die," said Scrooge, "they had better do it, and decrease the surplus population."

Embedded:

In Stave One Dickens presents Scrooge as a man who does not care about the poor and feels like he doesn't have any responsibility towards them. He suggests that "if they would rather die", then "they had better do it, and decrease the surplus population".

It may seem like only a small change to embed the quotation, but it will help the examiner to follow what you are saying more easily and will make your paragraph "flow".

Improving your written expression

AO1, the first assessment objective, talks about the "style" of your writing. It must be formal and critical, meaning that it should feel balanced and not too over-the-top.

Sentence starters to avoid and sophisticated substitutions

When you use the same sentence starters and phrases in an essay, it can feel stiff and unnatural to read. These are some simple changes you can make so that your essay sounds more formal and it will help you to vary your response:

Avoid overusing…	Use instead…
"Dickens **presents** Scrooge as…"	<ul><li>Dickens **illustrates** Scrooge as…</li><li>Dickens **portrays** Scrooge as…</li><li>Dickens **depicts** Scrooge as…</li><li>Dickens **reveals** Scrooge as… to the reader</li><li>Dickens **paints** Scrooge as…</li></ul>
"This **shows**"	<ul><li>This **suggests**</li><li>This **indicates**</li><li>This **implies**</li><li>This **infers**</li></ul>
"I think/I feel/I believe" **(never use "I" in an essay)**	<ul><li>It could be argued that…</li><li>The reader is left with the impression that…</li><li>The reader is positioned to feel that…</li><li>This could be interpreted as…</li></ul>

"The character represents"	<ul><li>The character **symbolises**…</li><li>The character **embodies**…</li><li>The character **reflects**…</li><li>The character **epitomises**…</li><li>The character **typifies**…</li><li>The character **exemplifies**…</li></ul>

Joining ideas and paragraphs together

If you start every single paragraph with the same word or in the same way, then it will get boring for the examiner.

1. Use adding and contrasting connectives to make connections between your paragraphs and improve the fluency of your writing.
   Adding connectives: 'In addition', 'Moreover', 'Furthermore', 'Similarly', 'As well as', 'Consequently'.
   Contrasting connectives: 'In contrast', 'However', 'Alternatively', 'On the other hand', 'Whereas'.

2. Add signposts for the examiner at the beginning of your paragraphs to let them know the part of the text you will be talking about.
   Signposts: 'At the beginning of the novella', 'Later on, in Stave Three', 'Finally', 'Eventually', 'In conclusion'.

Using evaluative adjectives

Just like in English Language, you may wish to make a judgement about how successful the author has been in achieving their purpose. This is another way of achieving the "critical style" that AO1 sets out. You could do this by using the following adjectives:

Adjective	Example
Skilful/Skilfully	Dickens **skilfully** uses the character of Scrooge to…
Subtle/Subtly	The use of … is a **subtle** hint that…
Pivotal	This **pivotal** moment in the novella means the reader is positioned to feel…
Effective	This is an **effective** method employed by Dickens to…
Striking	This **striking** image serves to…
Challenging	This is a **challenging** moment in the novella that allows the reader to…
Central concern	The theme of… is a **central concern** to the novella.
Significant	This is particularly **significant** because…

Some further sophisticated analytical tips

1. Analysing an alternative interpretation:

    - The phrase could also be interpreted as revealing…

2. Analysing the combined effect of several techniques together:

    - The writer uses _____ coupled with_____ to illustrate…

3. Tracking how key ideas are developed through a text:

    - This idea is further developed when…

4. Deepening the analysis of a character/theme:

    - On the exterior _____, yet on further inspection of the character the reader sees…

    - At first glance _____; however, on closer inspection the reader learns…

Making the main paragraph even more analytical

Let's look back at the example main paragraph from earlier and see all of these written expressions in action:

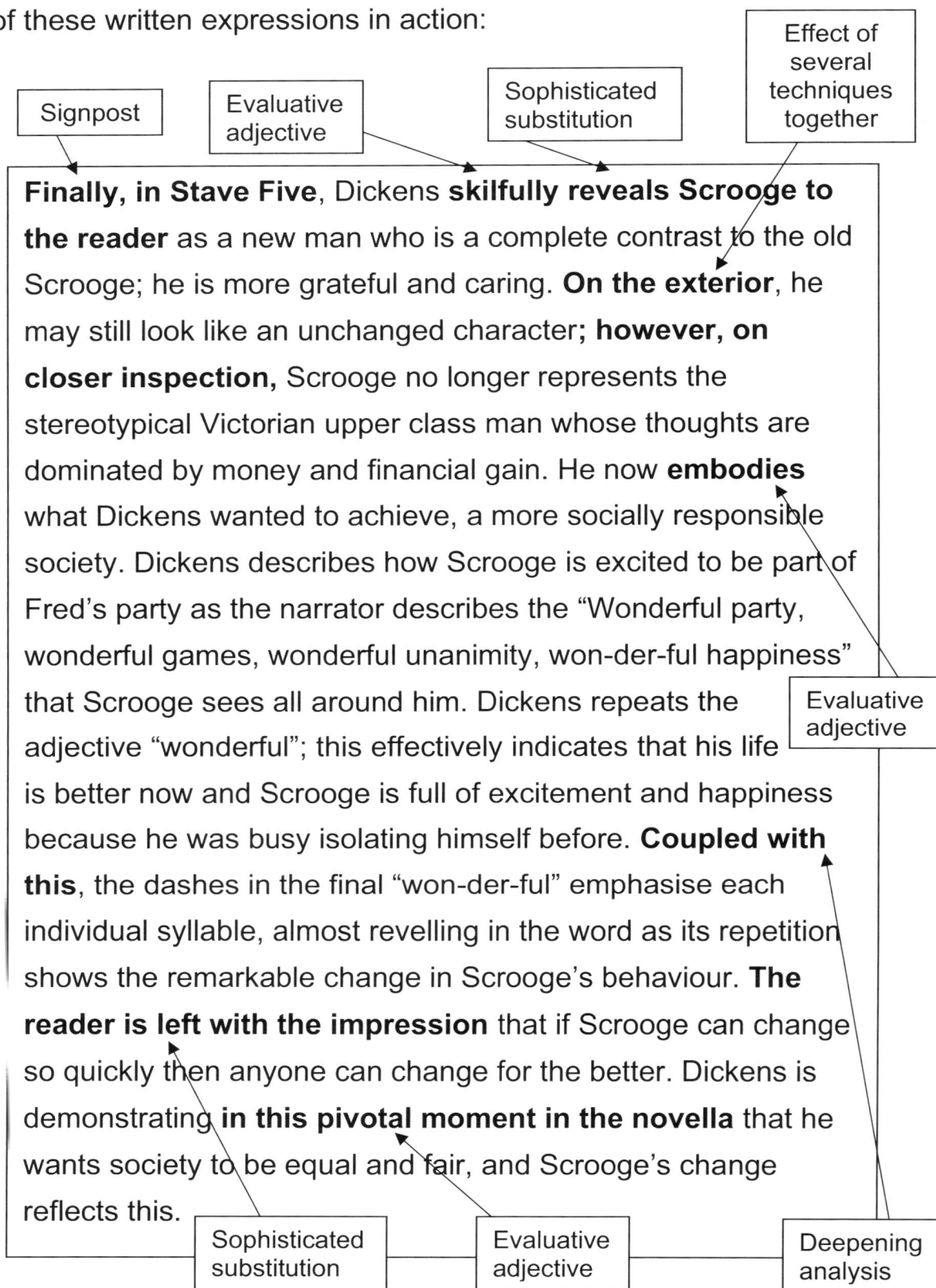

| Signpost | Evaluative adjective | Sophisticated substitution | Effect of several techniques together |

Finally, in Stave Five, Dickens **skilfully reveals Scrooge to the reader** as a new man who is a complete contrast to the old Scrooge; he is more grateful and caring. **On the exterior**, he may still look like an unchanged character; **however, on closer inspection,** Scrooge no longer represents the stereotypical Victorian upper class man whose thoughts are dominated by money and financial gain. He now **embodies** what Dickens wanted to achieve, a more socially responsible society. Dickens describes how Scrooge is excited to be part of Fred's party as the narrator describes the "Wonderful party, wonderful games, wonderful unanimity, won-der-ful happiness" that Scrooge sees all around him. Dickens repeats the adjective "wonderful"; this effectively indicates that his life is better now and Scrooge is full of excitement and happiness because he was busy isolating himself before. **Coupled with this**, the dashes in the final "won-der-ful" emphasise each individual syllable, almost revelling in the word as its repetition shows the remarkable change in Scrooge's behaviour. **The reader is left with the impression** that if Scrooge can change so quickly then anyone can change for the better. Dickens is demonstrating **in this pivotal moment in the novella** that he wants society to be equal and fair, and Scrooge's change reflects this.

| Evaluative adjective |

| Sophisticated substitution | Evaluative adjective | Deepening analysis |

~ Progress and revision check answers ~

Background information

1. Dickens believed that charity was important all year round.

2. Dickens worked in a factory which is where he first became sympathetic to the suffering of factory workers.

3. Dickens was inspired to write A Christmas Carol after he read a government report about children's terrible workplace experiences.

4. The time period when Britain's primary economy changed from agriculture to factory work was called The Industrial Revolution.

5. The consequences of rapid population growth in London were that factory owners made a lot of money but the factory workers experienced terrible poverty.

6. Thomas Robert Malthus was the economist who believed starvation would solve poverty.

7. The government passed the 1834 New Poor Law to attempt to control poverty.

8. Sabbatarianism is the belief that Sunday is a holy day when no one should work.

9. The Victorians enjoyed reading ghost stories.

10. Christmas cards, crackers, carols and Christmas dinner were all Christmas traditions that grew in popularity at the end of the 19th century.

The novella – summary and analysis

1. The story begins on Christmas Eve.

2. The young Scrooge was left alone at school at Christmas time.

3. The two children that the Ghost of Christmas Present reveals from under his robes are called Ignorance and Want.

4. The occupations of the three people who sell the dead man's possessions are a charwoman, a laundress and an undertaker's assistant.

5. Scrooge sends a turkey – the biggest in the bakery – in a cab to the Cratchits on Christmas Day.

6. The 'fog and darkness' at the beginning of the story represent ignorance about the reality of poverty and how it is everywhere in society.

7. Scrooge tries to hide the light that is shining from the Ghost of Christmas Past to prevent the ghost from showing him any more of his past behaviour and actions, which has upset him greatly.

8. Dickens juxtaposes the Christmas celebrations with the description of the children Ignorance and Want to emphasise the contrast between what Christmas is like for those living in poverty and what is it like for wealthy people who are celebrating with their families and with plenty of food.

9. The use of dramatic irony builds tension because the reader is waiting for Scrooge to realise that the dead man is him, and to see his reaction and whether this will persuade him to change.

10. The use of pathetic fallacy in the final stave represents how Scrooge now has an enlightened attitude towards helping those in poverty.

The characters

1. Marley died seven years before the novella begins.

2. The character Tiny Tim represents the reality behind the issue of poverty in society and shows how the poor are real people with real feelings.

3. Fred believes that being kind, forgiving and charitable is important at Christmas time.

4. The Ghost of Christmas Past asks Scrooge questions to prompt answers from him to help him work out what he needs to do to become a better person.

5. The Ghost of Christmas Present's torch spreads happiness and stops people arguing, showing how Christmas is a time of forgiveness and goodwill.

6. The face of the Ghost of Christmas Yet To Come is hidden to represent how we cannot see what will happen in the future.

7. Fred and Fan are similar because Fred wants to include Scrooge in his family Christmas celebrations and Fan begged their father to bring Scrooge home from school to be with their family at Christmas time.

8. Mr Fezziwig and Scrooge are different because Mr Fezziwig is kind, generous and values all of his employees, however Scrooge

doesn't pay Bob much and makes him work in freezing cold conditions.

9. Scrooge doesn't feel he should be charitable in Stave One because he believes he is busy enough making money with his own business and shouldn't have to worry about helping other people, especially those he feels are lazy. He also believes he already helps them through paying taxes to the government, who provide food and shelter for the poor in the workhouses.

10. Scrooge's generosity in Stave Five shows that he is now aware that he must have more social responsibility and help those less fortunate than himself. He realises he should be a more generous employer and give to charity to support those living in poverty.

Themes

1. The Ghost of Christmas Present personifies 'the Christmas Spirit'.

2. Mr Fezziwig holds a Christmas party for his employees.

3. The laundress says Scrooge should blame himself for his isolation when he dies.

4. Fred, Fan, Belle, the Cratchits, the miners, the lighthouse men and the sailors are all people, or groups of people, who value family.

5. Belle says Scrooge is afraid of poverty, which makes his attitude to those who live in poverty even more shocking because he knows what it is like to fear it.

6. Mr Fezziwig, Fred, Fan, Belle, the Cratchits, the thieves, the wealthy businessmen and the family who owe Scrooge money are all people who teach Scrooge a lesson.

7. Dickens believes helping to prevent 'Ignorance' is more important than responding to 'Want' to help people in poverty because if they are educated they can get better jobs and earn more money. Then they can buy food, clothes and better living conditions for themselves. However, if people give the poor the things they need it will only help them temporarily and they will keep needing more charitable donations in future.

8. Scrooge hates Christmas and believes it is not worth celebrating because people are growing older and don't make money from Christmas. Fred values Christmas and believes it is a time for family and friends and for being kind and generous towards those who have little money.

9. Scrooge's childhood was lonely as he was left at school at Christmas time by his father until Fan persuaded him to bring Scrooge home. Belle's children enjoy being in each other's company at their family home and have a great affection for their parents, who love them greatly in return.

10. Dickens uses Tiny Tim's death to show the reality of what could happen to children living in poverty who do not have access to good health care. He aims to shock the reader so that they feel more sympathy towards the poor by seeing the consequences of poverty for an innocent child and their family, which he hopes will make them become more charitable.

Form, structure and language

1. The form of A Christmas Carol is a novella.

2. A stave is another word for a stanza or verse, which is associated with carols.

3. At the climax of the novel, the name on the gravestone is revealed to be Scrooge's.

4. The name of the structure describing the way Stave Five mirrors Stave One is called a symmetrical structure.

5. Dickens uses an intrusive narrator, which allows him to comment on the characters and their actions and to make moral and political points without taking responsibility as the narrator, even though he is the author.

6. Dickens creates a sinister atmosphere through his use of metaphors.

7. The use of pathetic fallacy represents Scrooge's transformation from a cold, unfeeling character to someone who takes responsibility for the poor.

8. Dickens personifies food to make it seem alive and like it wants to be part of the Christmas celebrations.

9. The similes show that Scrooge's character is transformed and that he is happy and youthful because he has the opportunity to make amends.

10. Dickens uses lists of adjectives to make his descriptions have more impact than if just one adjective had been used.